CREATING COOL WEB PAGES

Lynda Tourloukis

Publications International, Ltd.

Lynda Tourloukis is a freelance Web site and graphic designer who constructs, operates, and maintains Internet sites. She also teaches children and adults the basics of creating and designing Web pages.

Illustrations: Rémy Simard

Louis Weber, CEO
Publications International, Ltd.
7373 North Cicero Avenue
Lincolnwood, Illinois 60712

Permission is never granted for commercial purposes.

Manufactured in China.

8 7 6 5 4 3 2 1

ISBN: 0-7853-4466-7

Contents

Introduction

THE INTERNET has exploded in popularity in recent years. It seems as if it's everywhere! But did you know that one of the best things about the Internet is that kids just like you can join in on the fun? You can create your very own site on the World Wide Web. It can be about pretty much anything—your family, your school, your favorite sport, whatever *you* want.

Part of what makes the Web so cool is that it lets people use two parts of their brains—the creative part and the scientific part. Kids who work on Web pages are learning more about computers while they're having fun being creative. You, too, can get in on the fun of creating your own Web page. Maybe you want to make a page that gives people a sneak peek into your everyday life. Or maybe you want a Web page that just you and your closest friends would enjoy, full of inside jokes and funny stories. It's up to you!

So now you're ready to jump into the world of the Web and make your own Web pages. You have to take first things first: Just how do you actually make a Web site? There are a few different ways.

You can get in touch with someone who builds Web pages for a living and have him or her design one for you. This is quick and easy, but it can also cost a lot of money. Plus, you don't get to learn very much that way. And, it's not much fun!

If you want to make a Web page by yourself, but you don't want to spend time learning a whole lot of the technical stuff about

how it's done, you can do that, too. You can buy software called Web-authoring programs or HTML editors. These programs write all of the Web language so you don't have to. You use plain English to tell the program what you want your page to look like, and it changes that into the technical language that's needed to make a Web page. This can be a lot more fun than having someone else make the page for you, but you still don't get to learn a whole lot about how a Web page is built.

If you *really* want to understand what goes into making a Web page, you need to learn the basic language of the Web: **H**yper**T**ext **M**arkup **L**anguage (usually called HTML). That's where *Creating Cool Web Pages* comes in. This book shows you how to use HTML to build a page from the ground up.

Don't worry! HTML isn't as scary as it sounds. It's just a language that gives instructions to computers. The computer reads this language to know what to include on your Web page and how it should look on the screen. Learning HTML takes more time than using a Web-authoring program, but since you'll understand Web pages so well, you'll be able to change your Web information whenever you want.

Anyone can make a Web page with a few simple things:

- a computer with a modem
- an Internet Service Provider, or ISP (for an online connection)
- a Web browser like Microsoft Internet Explorer or Netscape Navigator
- a word processing program

It's as easy as that. Read on to learn how to get the most out of this book, and then you're all ready to start on your very own Web page adventure!

How to Use This Book

Creating Cool Web Pages is designed for kids like you who want to learn HTML and become a part of the World Wide Web.

You won't be alone on your journey into the new world of the Web. Cyber Sid will be along to help out. Sid's a robot with lots of Web smarts. He'll pop up from time to time to help guide you around, to define a confusing term, or to suggest some helpful hints. With Cyber Sid's help, you won't build just any old Web page...you'll build a *cool* one.

Before you create your Web page, it's important to know about some of the dangers that are out there on the World Wide Web. Chapter 1 provides Internet safety tips that will help you surf the Web and download programs safely. It also tells you what kinds of stuff may be hurtful to you or your visitors if you put them on your Web page.

Chapter 2 helps you begin your cyber journey. It explains the Internet and the World Wide Web and shows how a Web page plays a part in them.

Once you understand more about the Web, you can become the architect or planner of your page. Chapter 3 will help. Planning the design of your Web page involves some decision-making. Your ideas need to be organized a bit, and you need to start creating a fun design. Luckily, Cyber Sid has a good eye for design and organization and can give you some great tips.

Now's the fun part—the page construction. As the construction engineer, you need to put on your virtual hard hat and learn the step-by-step process of building a page. Chapter 4 will teach you how to write and speak HTML. It might seem confusing, but stick with it, and try everything on your computer before getting too frustrated. You'll be an HTML pro in no time!

Once you're comfortable, move on to Chapter 5. It introduces you to some of the more fun Web page elements, such as adding music. This will not only make your Web page more interesting— it'll make it cool!

Before anyone can see your page, you have to publish it. That means you have to put it on the Web. Chapter 6 will tell you how to do this.

As you work on the Web, you'll see lots of words and phrases that will confuse you at first. Go to Chapter 7 to learn what they mean. This chapter is a handy, one-stop reference section to remind you of all that you have learned. Best of all, the resource chapter has lots of useful Web addresses.

OK, now you're ready to go. Put on your virtual hard hat, introduce yourself to Cyber Sid, and get ready to enter the Cyber Zone.

Net Safety for Kids

HE INTERNET can be such a fun place for kids! There's so much to see and do. But there is danger online, too. That doesn't mean that the Internet is a scary place. It's not. But that does mean that you should be careful when you are online. Play it safe while you are surfing the Web looking for ideas or goodies for your Web page. This chapter will explain how you can do that.

Staying Safe Online

You know from reading the newspaper and watching TV that there are some people in the world who do some not-so-nice things. There are lots and lots of really great people online, but there are some of those not-so-nice people, too. Your parents and this book can help you with some safety tips. However, it's up to you to make good choices that will keep you safe and make your Web experience the happy one it should be.

- Don't give out your real name, address, or phone number to a stranger on the Internet. It might feel like you know the person, but you don't really know what he or she is like in real life.
- An e-mail name makes you anonymous. That means no one knows who you really are. It's kind of like a disguise. Some-times adults even pretend to be young kids online so they can try to become your friends. These sorts of people aren't your friends. Remember, just because people tell you something online about themselves, that doesn't mean it's true.

- Never arrange to meet someone you've met online. Even though you may feel like you know him or her, this person is really still a stranger.
- If you are chatting online and someone says or does something that makes you uncomfortable, tell someone—a chat room supervisor, your ISP host, or a trusted adult.
- If you find yourself at an adult site or one that makes you uncomfortable, hit the Back button in the upper-left corner of your screen to leave right away.
- Never, ever give out your password. No one should ever ask you for this online. If someone does, it's a sure sign that he or she is up to no good.

Making Your Site Safe

You should think about safety when you're designing your Web site, too. For example, only use pictures and graphics that are right for your viewers. Don't use any pictures that will embarrass or offend them.

And don't use bad language. Viewers are your guests. The Golden Rule is also true in cyberspace: Treat others the way that you would want to be treated.

Don't list your phone number or address on your site. If there is some reason to put an address on the page, ask your parents to rent a post office box. It's not much money, and that way your mail from Web viewers will go to the post office for you to pick up. Then people won't know your real address.

You can list your site with a search engine like Yahoo (www. yahoo.com) or Lycos (www.lycos.com), but think about it first. A search engine tells lots and lots of people about your page. You should decide first if you want strangers to look at your personal site. However, if you have an informational site, this may be just what you want. Talk it over with your parents before you launch the page. See Chapter 6 for more information.

The Dangers of Downloading

You don't have to be careful online just for yourself. Your computer can get hurt by some stuff you find online, too. Sometimes you'll **download** information from the Web, and you'll pick up a nasty little virus along with it. Yuck! This could be big trouble for your computer. Just like viruses make people sick, computer viruses can make computers sick. Viruses can make computers work incorrectly or—worse—they can totally ruin the computer!

You can avoid these little nasties with a few precautions. First, know your source. There are billions of pages on the Web, and some of them are set out to do harm. You're careful when you're out someplace new in the real world, right? It's the same on the Web. If you're

WEB WORD

When you **download** information, you get information, files, or programs from another computer on the Web and electronically bring them into your computer so you can use them.

on a site that you don't know very well, be careful. Also, think about these things:

- Has the site been around awhile? Sites that harm people don't usually last too long. As soon as people find out about them, law agencies like the FBI shut them down.
- It's a good sign if the Web site has a physical location, such as a retail store. That can show that the site is serious about what it says.
- Sites that have downloads should also have a phone number and an address for you to ask them questions. If there isn't a number or an address, the site might not be safe.
- Does the site have a secure connection? If you want to buy a program online, your parents might have to use their credit card to pay for it. But first you want to be sure that no one

can steal the credit card number while it's online. A site is safe for credit cards when you see a small locked padlock or an unbroken key in the lower-left corner of your browser screen. If the lock is shown as open or the image of the key is broken, then this site might not be safe to send credit card or other personal information.

How Viruses Are Spread

A file that has an .exe or .com at the end of its name is a program. This is the way computer viruses are spread. They ride in with other programs and when you run them, the viruses begin to go through your computer and hurt things.

Before you use any downloaded program, run it through your antivirus software first. (Remind your parents to update the antivirus software regularly. New viruses are always popping up.)

You should also be careful when you pass floppy disks from computer to computer. A floppy disk that is infected with a virus can pass it on to the computer of anyone who uses that disk.

Viruses can also be spread by e-mail attachments. If you get a download by e-mail, make sure you know who sent it to you. Also, check to see if it looks like something they would send you. If it looks weird, don't open the program. Ask an adult to look at it, too. You should delete any unsafe e-mails and then empty the computer's trash/recycle bin. (If you are using Microsoft Office programs, disable them from automatically opening your e-mail. They could open an infected .exe or .com program before you stop it.)

Welcome to the Internet and the World Wide Web!

WHEN THE INTERNET first started back in the late 1960s, only high-tech-type people used it. This was back when computers were *so* huge that one filled an entire room. Computer scientists thought it would make things easier if scientists and researchers could talk to each other through the computer.

Those first few years of "talking" through a computer didn't look anything like e-mail or the World Wide Web! To talk over the computer, people had to use a complicated programming language that was all just words and numbers (no pictures).

Plus, only a very few people were able to use that first computer network. Most people had never even heard of computers.

Then, in the 1970s, a system called **G**raphical **U**ser **I**nterface (GUI) was developed. GUI (often pronounced gooey) is what lets computer users see pictures and colors over the Internet. It also lets them click on links to get and send information over the Net. Ever since GUI, computers and the Internet are much easier to use. And have they ever become popular! Now, only a short time later, most everyone can get on the Internet. They can all be *part* of the Internet, too. Now that's progress!

BTA—BEWARE THE ACRONYM

An acronym (A-cruh-nim) is when people take the first letter (or letters) of each word in a long phrase to make one short word. For example, people take **A**s **S**oon **A**s **P**ossible and make it ASAP.

In case you haven't noticed, computer people just love to use acronyms. That's because there are many long phrases related to the Internet. To make them easier to say and faster to write or speak, everyone uses acronyms instead. One of the best examples of a Web acronym is one you've already learned. It's **H**yper**T**ext **M**arkup **L**anguage, which people shorten to HTML. GUI (**G**raphical **U**ser **I**nterface) is another Web acronym.

So many Internet acronyms may be confusing at first, but after you use them a bit and start to understand what they mean, it will get easier. And don't forget that lots of Web acronyms and their meanings are listed in the glossary of this book. You can always check there if you become confused.

So, is there a difference between the Internet and the World Wide Web? Actually, there's a big difference. The World Wide Web is just a part of the Internet. The Web is actually something that you use on the Internet. Think of it like this: The Internet is like hardware, such as computers and cable wire, and the World Wide Web is like software programs that you put on your computer.

Still confused? Don't worry! Read on to get a better idea of the differences between the Net and the Web.

THE INTERNET

The Internet is made up of computers that are connected through wires, fiber optics (fancy wires), and satellite transmissions. A computer can communicate with other computers in the world because of this link. The computer sends information along the fancy, high-tech wires—just the same way your voice travels along telephone wires to reach someone else.

Did you ever wonder how a computer sends out all of that information? It does that through its modem. A modem is a small piece of hardware that is installed in your computer (or some modems are outside of the computer). When you are connected online, the information you send out and receive comes over the telephone line. Your modem switches the information into a format that your computer understands. Your computer then changes it into the messages that you see on your screen.

THE WORLD WIDE WEB

The World Wide Web is a part of the Internet. It's best thought of as a huge (*very, very* huge) encyclopedia made up of billions of pages. But unlike an encyclopedia, the Web is not organized in a clear way. This sometimes makes it hard to find all that is out there.

Every time you look for a Web page, your computer is looking up an address called a **U**niform **R**esource **L**ocator (URL). URL is really just a fancy term for the address of a specific Web page.
A URL could look like this: www.vegasthecat.com. Another Web page on that same site could have a URL that looks like this: www.vegasthecat.com/photos.html.

You're probably asking yourself, "What does all this www. and .com stuff mean?" That's just the way the computer understands an address.

First, the computer looks at the www followed by a dot (www.), and it knows that it should look for this address on the **W**orld **W**ide **W**eb.

Then it looks for the name of the site and finds that it's called vegasthecat. The computer now has to figure out where to look for the page on the Web, so it reads the extension at the end of the URL. Extension is a big word for adding something to the end of a thing. The extension for this site is the .com at the end of the address.

The Web uses many extensions at the ends of its addresses. The .com on www.vegasthecat.com tells the computer that this URL is a business, company, or personal page. You may also notice other types of extensions when you are out surfing, such as:

- *.net* This is a network of computers that are all linked together.
- *.org* This is an organization, such as the Girl Scouts or the American Cancer Society.
- *.gov* This is a government address, such as www.whitehouse. gov. Bet you can guess who lives there!
- *.edu* This is an educational address. For example, The Ohio State University has a Web address of www.ohio-state.edu.

Now that you know that Web pages have addresses, do you know where they live?

Where a Web Page Lives

If a Web page has an address, then it must have a home, right? A Web page lives on a host computer (also called a server computer). A host computer is like an apartment building. An apartment building owner lets you rent space in his or her building for a price.

A host computer's owner is called a provider. Just like a building owner, a provider lets you rent space for a price. This time, though, you're paying to have a Web page "live" on the provider's computer. When you type in the page's address, your computer sends out a message to the provider's computer and asks the Web page out for a visit.

This is where a browser comes in. When you sit down to your computer to surf the Net, you begin by clicking on your **I**nternet **S**ervice **P**rovider, or ISP (there's another one of those acronyms). Some popular ISPs are America Online and Earthlink. When you log on to your ISP, you use a browser to view Web pages. Some ISPs, such as America Online, have browsers built right in, so you might not even know that you're using one.

For other ISPs, such as Earthlink, you have to use a browser like Microsoft Internet Explorer or Netscape Navigator. These browsers have their own icons on the desktop of your computer. Click on the icon to open the browser software and get into your ISP. Together, the browser and the ISP will make the Web available for you to see.

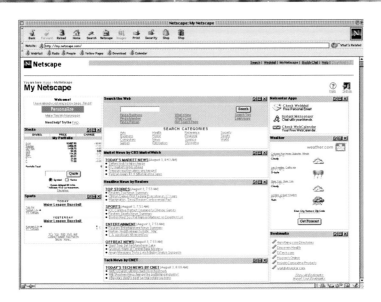

How Does the Browser Work?

Suppose you send a party invitation to a friend. You have to write or type out the address on the envelope and mail it. Once the invitation arrives at the address, a family member might see it in the mailbox and pass it along to your friend. If your friend can come to your party, he or she will show up at your house at the time you asked. But if your friend is ill or busy and can't come to the party, he or she will probably call or send a message to say why.

Using a browser to surf the Web is kind of like that. On the computer, when you type in an address or URL for a Web page in your browser, it's the same as sending that invitation to your friend.

In this case, when you type in the address, your browser sends a message to the host computer that the Web page lives on (just like the invitation arrived by mail at your friend's house). The host passes the message along to the Web page, saying that you are calling to ask it out. If the page is feeling well and doesn't have any problems, the host computer will pull up an image of the page and display it on your computer screen. You view the page, and everyone is happy.

Of course, just like sometimes your friends can't come to your parties, sometimes Web pages can't come out, either. When your browser shows you an error message, this is like when your friend calls to tell you that he or she can't come to the party. The host is sending a message to your computer that the Web page can't come out to play just then. This can happen for lots of reasons—maybe someone's fixing a problem on the page, or it's possible that the page doesn't live with that host anymore.

Your browser will be important when you start making your own Web page, too. When you're working on your page, you'll want to open it in your browser often to see how it looks so far. When you do this, you'll be working in "offline" mode. Offline means that you aren't connected to the Internet.

When you open your browser to check the Web page you're making, don't log on with your ISP. If your ISP automatically asks you to sign on when you open the browser, just click on the X in the small gray box at the top of the sign-in box. This should close the sign-in box but keep the browser open. (Some browsers may also ask you if you want to work in an offline mode. If it does this, just click Yes.)

THE DIFFERENCE BETWEEN A WEB PAGE AND A WEB SITE

People talk about Web sites and Web pages a lot. Are they the same thing? Not exactly. A Web page is a single actual page that you look at online through your browser.

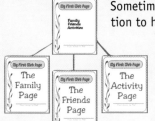

Sometimes, though, a Web page has too much information to have on one page and still keep it easy to use. That's when a Web designer breaks it up into many linked Web pages. All of the Web pages that are linked together under one shared address are called a Web site.

Of course, just to be a little more confusing, even a single Web page with an address can be called a Web site. Anytime a page is on the Web and people can get to it, that's considered a Web site. The term Web site means the entire package of a Web page (or Web pages) and its address.

Planning and Designing Your Web Pages

MOST OF YOU probably have some kind of idea of what sort of Web page or site you would like to develop. The most important thing to consider in putting together a Web page is deciding just what you want it to say to the world. This means that your Web site needs to have a purpose. Let's take a look at some ideas that you can use to get the most out of your Web site.

Hot Ideas for Cool Web Pages

DEVELOPING A PERSONAL PAGE
This is probably one of the most popular Web design ideas for kids. A personal page usually includes information about the coolest person you know—you!

A personal Web page lets you tell the entire world about all kinds of hot topics in your life: friends, family, hobbies, clubs, activities, games, music, sports...anything that excites you. Just think of things you like, and you're on your way!

CREATING A GROUP OR CLUB PAGE

This page has information about a group or club that you belong to, that you want to start, or that you just find interesting. For example, you could make a page that talks about:

- a youth service group
- an environmental club
- your school class
- art, drama, or music groups
- a sports team
- your dance class

You don't have to already be involved in a group to create a group page. How about creating a page with an online treehouse that's a secret club for kids just like you?

HOSTING A GAMES PAGE

What goes together better than kids and games? You can make a great page full of fun stuff—games, jokes, puzzles, and riddles. And there's plenty of information online to help you put this kind of page together. Some Web sites let you download games, jokes, and even music so that you can use them on your own site.

MAKING A PROJECTS PAGE

If you've worked hard on a special project for school, now you can show it off to the whole world! You could include pictures to show everyone all about what you did in the project.

You don't have to do just one of these examples. Your Web site could have a Web page that has games and talks about a club you belong to. Now that you've got an idea about the types of things to include on your site, it's time to get organized!

Making an Outline

An outline is the first step in putting all your ideas in one place. It's also a great way to figure out how you want to organize your site.

But don't worry about any organizing just yet. Start by writing down a way to welcome the world to your site, and list all of the ideas that you want to include on your site. Next, make each of the ideas a category, and list things about each category that you would like to talk about.

Now's the time to start setting up your outline. Decide which thing you want to talk about first on the site, and that's what should go closer to the beginning of the outline. Now, write up your own outline. Remember, a category with a Roman numeral comes first. Next, write down your ideas about the categories. These ideas should have a capital letter before them.

I. Welcome
    A. Introduce myself and the site
    B. Say what my site will be about
    C. Show interesting artwork or pictures

II. My Family
    A. Give descriptions of family members
    B. Tell what makes my family interesting
    C. Include photos

III. My Friends
    A. Tell fun things about my friends
    B. Talk about what we like to do together
    C. Include pictures or drawings

IV. My Activity Page
    A. Explain any groups/clubs I belong to
    B. Tell about school activities
    C. Talk about my favorite sports

Once you create your outline, you should have a better idea of what you want on your Web site. Remember that you can add as much or as little detail as you'd like. You can even combine ideas, like putting the information for friends and activities in one section.

One word of advice: Don't feel like you *have* to stick to this outline. You can always make changes as you go along. The outline is just a starting point. Once you are better at HTML, you can add all kinds of things. This is *your* Web site, so have fun, be creative, and always remember: You're the **Webmaster**!

Now that you have a rough outline, it's time to put on your artist's cap and start thinking about what the site will look like.

Design Basics

If you look at the sample outline, you'll see that there are four categories. You could make that really interesting by creating a separate Web page for each category and linking them all together.

Of course, you also could just include all of the information on one very long page, but it's much more cyber-cool to have links on your site. You're going to learn all about linking in future chapters, so let's just go ahead and make four separate, linked pages.

Now it's time to get a better idea of how you want these pages to look. You need to decide where to put the text

WEB WORDS

The **Webmaster** is the person who is in charge of creating and/or maintaining a Web site.

and where to put any images or pictures. The best way to do this is by going back to the basics—old-fashioned paper and pencil.

Get out four sheets of paper, and draw a square box on each. Each piece of paper will show one of your Web pages. Draw smaller boxes on the "Web page" where you think your art would look nice. (You could even draw in what the art looks like.) Next, add in the text on each page. To make things easier, you can just draw a box and put the word "text" inside it to show what it will be. Use your outline as a guide for what you want to include. How do you like how they look? Keep working until you are happy with your designs.

Be creative, and don't be afraid to try something new. This is just a rough plan. It can be changed as you go along if something doesn't work out like you wanted it to. Remember, you're the artist, and you get to be in charge of what goes on the site. That's part of the fun of being a Web designer!

> **WHAT IS A LINK?**
> A link—a shortened term for hyperlink—is usually a word on a Web page that is underlined and high-lighted a different color (usually blue). You can click on the high-lighted word with your mouse to "jump" from the page you are on to another page.

Elements of Good Design

There are certain design tricks you can do to make sure that your site will look its best. Now that you have drawn out a sketch of your design plan, let's take a look at what exactly makes a good design.

The rule of thumb with Web design is to keep it simple. You've probably seen some sites that have way too much information crammed on their pages. That makes it very hard to read, and it makes the page move slower. Don't forget that in Cyber City, the action is fast, and slow-moving pages are old news. And you don't want to be old news, right?

The design of your Web site represents you, so make sure it shows how good your style is. Ask yourself a few questions while you're creating your design:

- Are the colors so bright that things are hard to read?
- Does the text type and size fit on the page? Does it look good?
- Are the graphics, photos, and images right for your readers? Are they the right size? Can you tell what they are?
- Can you move easily around the site? Have you linked all of the pages?

Now That's a Good Design!

Sometimes the best way to learn about good design is just to see it. Go to www.vegasthecat.com to see an example of a great layout (and to see some really fun stuff). This site has all of the elements that make up a well-designed site.

First, it has a purpose. It's about a cat named Vegas. The purpose is to tell a fun story about a day in the life of this cat. Its design is simple, yet it's still nice to look at. It doesn't have too much, but what it does have, it uses well.

The Vegas site also has a theme. Many design elements repeat on every page. That shows you that it all goes together. It also shows how much the designer thought about the layout—that stuff takes planning!

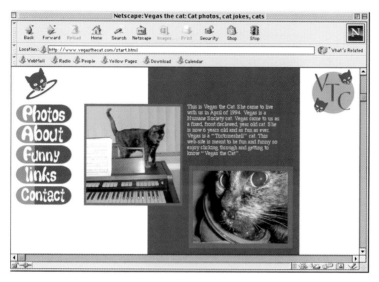

Now think about the design questions you just read about, and look at the site again. The choices for background colors are perfect. The colors are soft, so the information and photos stand out. The text and images blend well and suit the topic. It has just the right amount of images and text. The navigation is good. You can go easily to the next page, go back to the previous page, or link to any page at any time.

Chapters 4 and 5 will talk more about good design. You'll learn more design ideas and see more examples of cool designs there. For now, though, it's time to dive into the HTML pool. Just follow your pal Cyber Sid, and jump on in!

TECHNO TIP

First list all your design ideas, and don't worry if there are a lot. Once you get started making your page, you'll soon find out what you can include and what you should leave out until you're better at HTML. Just keep your outline and drawings in a safe place, and you can always go back to them when you have more cyber skills.

Design Done Delightfully

To make your site the eye-catching attraction you want it to be, mix a large dose of creativity with a big pinch of common sense. The key to good design is just to follow a few basic rules. Avoid overdone and half-baked ideas by following these:

- Simplicity is the key to understanding. This means that everyone will understand your page better if you keep it simple. Don't complicate your page with too much text, color, or graphics.
- Use good color combinations. Remember that other people will be viewing your site and need to be able to easily read it. Some color choices make that difficult. If you use a bold or bright background color, use a text that contrasts with it. That way, the text will stand out clearly.
- Limit the number of moving items on the page. A page that's overloaded with movement and blinking text and lots of activity is a viewer's nightmare. Make sure your design enhances the page—not ruins it!
- Keep file size in mind. Larger images create bigger files, and these will slow down your pages as they load. Viewers don't like to be kept waiting and will often leave rather than stick around.
- Be consistent in your design. If your viewer can tell that the links will be at the bottom on every page, they will be more likely to navigate through your entire site since it's so easy. If you move things around or keep changing color or text, your viewer might get confused.
- Consider these questions: Does your page have a purpose? Are you making the point you wanted? Does the site make sense? Keep these questions in mind as you design your site, and then review them again when you are finished.

Cool and Creative Kids Online

Now that you know the rules, it's time to hit the Web for some inspiration. Checking out the work of others is one way to help you learn about design. It also helps you to decide just what you want to put on your page and how you want it to look. There are so many great sites done by kids. These examples are just a few of them. They all include some good elements of design.

The first is Emma's Galaxy, which is at www.geocities.com/EnchantedForest/Pond/2571/index.htm. Emma uses a dark background, but she sets it off nicely with text colors that are easy to read. There's not a lot on her page, but what's there really shows her interests—dogs and her galaxy world.

Also check out Adam's Science Stuff, which is at www.scistuff.com. Adam's page is simple yet colorful and filled with fun. The animated parts of his design are great! The rest of the site is well designed and very interesting.

Visit Lissa Explains It All at www.lissaexplains.com. The colors on this site all complement each other and are consistent from page to page. The text information is well thought out. It's also arranged on the page in a nice way. The graphics are simple and help support the text. Aside from the design aspect, this site is a good example of respect for copyright and plagiarism issues, and the young author willingly shares her knowledge to help kids build Web pages.

Go look at Safety & Dangers of the Web at tqjunior.thinkquest.org/5210. This site is made by two 12-year-old girls. It's a nicely designed site with an important purpose. It teaches about kid safety on the Web. The girls have designed their page using darker background colors and lighter text. Simple images enhance the theme and purpose of the site. The content makes this another awesome contribution to kids online everywhere.

Your Step-by-Step Guide to HTML

YOU WILL NEED the following items to build your Web page:

- A computer. Any computer that can have an online connection will do.
- A modem and a phone line. Your parents can make sure that the phone line is hooked up to the computer and that a modem is installed. A modem is usually inside the computer, but there are also some that are hooked up outside of the computer.
- An Internet Service Provider (ISP). This is a company like America Online or CompuServe that connects the phone line from your home computer to the Internet.
- An Internet browser. A browser is software that lets you see the World Wide Web pages. Two popular ones are Microsoft Internet Explorer and Netscape Navigator. Some ISPs, such as AOL, have browsers built right into their systems.
- Editor software. Computers come with simple editor software. PCs have software called Notepad, and Macintosh computers have SimpleText. They are probably in the Accessories section of your computer. You use these programs to build your Web pages because they let you use only numbers, letters, and a few other keystrokes. Since HTML uses only those simple things, too, it's a perfect match.
- A 3½-inch floppy disk. Make sure you format it in the computer before you use it. Just put the disk in the disk drive, and the computer will format it if it needs to.

You're ready to begin as soon as you have all of these. When in doubt about what you do and don't have, just ask Mom or Dad.

Learning Some Basics

The following are some examples of terms you'll see in *Creating Cool Web Pages*. Look these over so you understand where different things are on your computer and what they do.

First, you should learn where the *Start button* is on the Windows computer system. It can take you to lots of your computer programs, including your Internet browser. Click on Start, and a menu will pop up. Choose Programs, and another menu will pop up. You can choose your browser from this menu to get online.

Another way to open your Internet connection is by clicking on the *Internet browser icon* on your computer desktop.

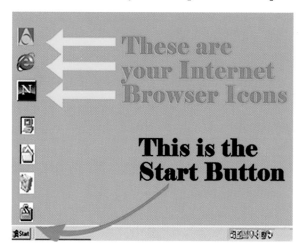

Every window on the computer has a *title bar* at the top. The title bar of the text editor shows the name of the file that you are working on. A file is made when you save anything you create on a computer. When you save something like a picture or a typed story, you have to give it a file name. Once you save the file, the name will show up on the title bar.

On the corner of every title bar are three buttons. The first is the minus sign, which is the *minimize button*. Minimize means to make smaller. Sometimes, you don't want to close a program, but you don't want it in the way while you work on something else. This is when you use the minimize button. Click on this button, and the program you are working on will become a small button at the bottom of your screen. When you want to go back to the file again, click on that small button. This will maximize the window. Maximize means to make bigger. The file will then be back to its original size.

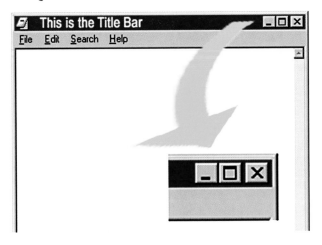

The second button in the title bar is either the *maximize button* or the *restore button*. When the screen is as big as it can get, the second button will be the restore button, which looks like two small squares on top of each other. Clicking on this will make the window a little smaller so you can see other parts of your desktop. This button comes in handy when you want to go back and forth between two or more programs. When the window doesn't fill the entire desktop, the second button in the title bar is the maximize button. The button looks like a square box. Click on it to make the window full size again.

The last button in the title bar has an X in it. This is the *close button*. You use this when you are done working with the file. It shuts down the file.

The *task bar* is the bar at the bottom of the screen. It displays the Start button. When you minimize a window, it will become a small button on the task bar. This means that the program hasn't been closed, and you can get back into it easily. It's just resting down there in the task bar!

If you are working on a Mac, you don't have to worry about maximizing and minimizing. You can keep all of the programs that you need open, and click back and forth between them.

Getting Started

First things first. Open your browser and your text editor. Do you remember how to open the browser? There are two ways: You can click on the icon on your desktop, or you can go to the Start button and find it in the Programs menu.

You should work on your Web page while your browser is offline. Offline means you aren't connected to the Internet. Don't sign on when the log-on screen for your Internet Service Provider (ISP) pops up. Click the X in the corner of the sign-on box. The browser window will stay open without connecting to the Internet. (The Microsoft Internet Explorer browser may ask you if you want to work in an offline mode. Click on Yes if this happens.)

Once the browser is opened, minimize it by clicking on the minus sign in the title bar at the top of the screen. Remember, your program is still open—it's just out of your way for now. See? There it is in the task bar at the bottom of the screen.

Next, open your text editor. You will use the text editor to create your pages. You want to use a text editor to type in the HTML because it doesn't add a lot of extra computer codes to the words. Most word processing programs add hidden codes that can screw up how the computer will read your HTML. That would be terrible after all of your hard work!

Most computers have Notepad (on PC computers) or SimpleText (on Macintosh computers). To find Notepad, click on the Start button in the lower-left corner of the screen. Click on the Programs folder. A menu will pop up. Click on Accessories from that menu. You should see Notepad in there. Click on it to open it. Macintosh users should double-click on the SimpleText icon to open the program.

Now you're ready to type. Click anywhere on the editor screen to begin. You will see a flashing cursor appear in the top left of the editor screen. Now you just have to know what to type.... Are you ready to learn some HTML?

On to the Code!

HTML is a language that is full of rules. Just like your parents have rules for you to live by, HTML has rules for computers to live by. If you don't follow the rules, the computer won't know how to read what you're telling it.

The first rule with HTML is that it must be inside of

WHY DO I NEED HTML?

HTML (HyperText Markup Language) is the computer language used by Web page designers. Of course, HTML isn't the only language of the Web. You can also mix other languages in with the HTML to have your Web site do different "tricks." But HTML is the most basic language, and you need to know it first before you can move on to bigger and better things.

angle brackets that look like this: < >. The left and right angle brackets are on your keyboard in the lower-right corner. They're on the same keys as the comma and the period. Press the Shift key, and hit one of the bracket keys to type it in.

All HTML code must be put inside angle brackets. This is how the computer knows what to read. The code and the angle brackets together are called a **tag**.

WEB WORDS

A **tag** is HTML code plus the angle brackets that go around it. For example, <HTML> at the top of the page is the opening HTML tag that tells the computer you will be using HTML code.

Before you start writing your Web page, you have to tell the computer that you are using HTML. To do this, you use an opening HTML tag. So type **<HTML>** at the top of your page. It comes before anything else. It is like the king of the page. It rules over everything else below it.

You have to use a tag to show the computer that you are starting to use HTML. So you probably have to find a way to show that you're done using HTML, too, right? That's when you use a closing tag. A forward slash mark (/) is used to make a closing tag. Put the forward slash in front of the letter or word inside the brackets, and it becomes a closing tag. The forward slash is on the lower-right corner of the keyboard. It's on the same key as the question mark.

To make an HTML closing tag, just put the forward slash in front of the letters. The tag looks like this: **</HTML>**. It tells the computer it can stop reading HTML. If you leave it off, your page will be blank.

The opening tag should go at the top of the page, and the closing tag should go at the bottom of the page. Other tags and all information that you add to your Web page must go between the opening HTML tag and the closing HTML tag.

These two tags are important, but so far all you really have is a blank Web page. Let's add more!

Tag—You're It!

There are a couple of important things to remember with tags. First, it's important to have the brackets on both sides and the slash mark for the closing tag. Also, it's best to use capital letters to write the code. This isn't really a rule: It's just a good habit. The capitals make it easier to read the code and find any mistakes.

The next tag you should know is the head tag: **<HEAD>**. The **<HEAD>** tag has an opening tag and a closing tag: **</HEAD>**. The **<HEAD>** tags tell the computer what to put in the header, or top, section of the Web page.

On the practice Web page you're going to work on, the only thing in the header will be the title of the page. The title tag goes

between the **<HEAD>** tags and looks like this: **<TITLE>**. There's also a closing **<TITLE>** tag: **</TITLE>**. Whatever you type inside these two tags will be the title of the page. The title of this page is "Welcome." That title won't show up on the Web page itself, but you will be able to see it in the browser's title bar. That is, if you were looking at this page on the Web, you would see Welcome in the title bar across the top of your browser screen.

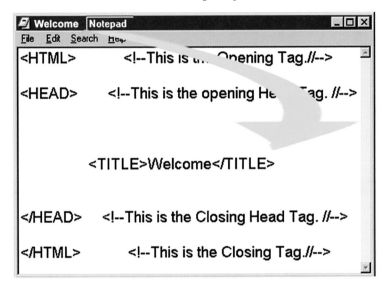

Did you notice how the **<HEAD>** tags go inside the **<HTML>** tags and the **<TITLE>** tags went inside the **<HEAD>** tags? This is called nesting. Nesting is when sets of tags are placed, or "nested," between another set of tags. Each set has an opening tag and a closing tag. The set of **<TITLE>** tags is nested inside of the set of **<HEAD>** tags, which are nested inside of the set of **<HTML>** tags.

Now let's add two more tags: the opening and closing **<BODY>** tags. The **<BODY>** tags are just like most other tags. The opening tag goes inside angle brackets: **<BODY>**. The closing tag goes inside the brackets and has a forward slash in front of it: **</BODY>**. As you can see, the **<BODY>** tags are nested inside of the **<HTML>** tags. In other words, the **<BODY>** tags are between the **<HTML>** tags.

The body section is the main part of a Web page. It holds most of the page's information, or content. All of the content of your Web page will go between the **<BODY>** tags.

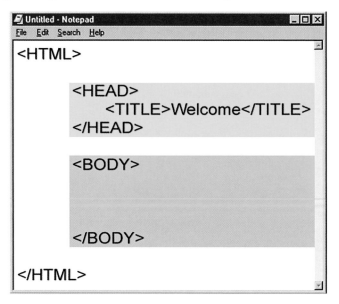

Let's begin with a welcome message. You'll want to give your viewers a big greeting when they visit your page. The top of the body section is the perfect place to do that. Try something like this for the body section:

<BODY>

Welcome to My Web Page, Cyber Dudes

</BODY>

That's a great message! It sure doesn't look very exciting, though. Why don't you try changing the size of the text to make it stand out more? To do this, you will use another set of tags called headings.

Headings should be used on any text you want to stand out. Headings make the page more organized and easier to read. That's always a good thing!

ADDING SOME HEADINGS

There are seven types of headings available for a Web page:

Heading 1

Heading 2

Heading 3

Heading 4

Heading 5

Heading 6

Heading 7

The good news is that the tags for headings are nice and short. Each heading tag is just a letter "H" with the heading number next to it. So the Heading 1 opening tag is **<H1>**, and the closing tag is **</H1>**. The others are

<H2> and **</H2>**

<H3> and **</H3>**

<H4> and **</H4>**

<H5> and **</H5>**

<H6> and **</H6>**

<H7> and **</H7>**

Now, let's add some headings to your code. Use the Heading 1 style, since that's the biggest. Of course, you will nest your heading code between the **<BODY>** tags. Type in:

<BODY>

<H1>Welcome to My Web Page, Cyber Dudes**</H1>**

</BODY>

Everything that is typed between the two **<H1>** tags will show up as Heading 1 size and style. It's very important to remember the closing tag. If you forget it, the rest of the text will all be in Heading 1 style. That would be a lot of big type. People who have bad eyesight might like it, though!

SAVING YOUR WORK

Now, the moment you've been waiting for—checking to see if your Web page really works. The first thing you need to do is save your work on a floppy disk. Put a formatted disk into the computer. In your text editor, click on File in the menu bar at the top of the screen. Then click on Save As. Now you have to tell the computer what you want to name the file and where to save it.

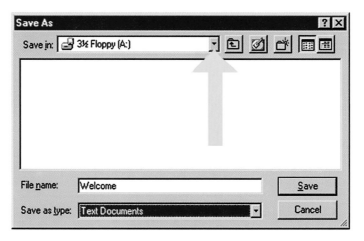

You want to save the file on the floppy disk, and you need to tell the computer that. On a PC, go to the Save in: box at the top of the Save As screen. Click on the small down arrow by the Save in: box, and choose 3½ Floppy (A:). The floppy disk is in the A: drive.

You also need to save the Web page as an HTML file. Click on the small black arrow next to the Save as type: box. From the drop-down menu, choose All Files (*.*). When you do this, the computer will be ready to save any type of file.

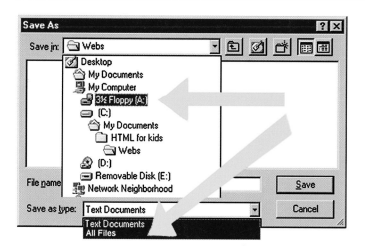

Now for the file name. Type Index.htm in the File name: box, and click on the Save button. The .htm extension is a file type. The L was dropped back when extensions had to be smaller and shorter.

To save your work on a Macintosh, click on Desktop in the Save As screen. Look for the disk's icon, and double-click on it. The computer will now save to the disk. Type Index.html in the file name area, and it's as easy as that!

Whether you have a Mac or a PC, it's very important to add the .htm or .html to the end of your file name. If you don't, the page won't show up on the browser. The computer won't know that it's an HTML file.

SHH! IT'S TOP-SECRET CODE

There's a way to add secret notes in HTML code that no one will be able to see on the page. They're called comment tags. The tag begins with <!-- and ends with //-->. Anything that you type between those cannot be seen on your Web page.

You use a comment tag to put in notes to yourself as you create your page. Say you want to add a picture of Uncle Joe to your family page, but you don't have the photo yet. Just put a set of comment tags in the code where you would put his picture. The tag could be something like: <!--Put a picture of Uncle Joe here//-->.

This probably seems long and hard right now. You'll be doing this a lot, though. Pretty soon, you'll be really good at it and will get it done quickly.

Once your machine has stopped saving, you will be ready to open the browser to view your page.

YOUR FIRST PEEK

First, minimize your text editor. (Remember? Click on the minus box in the upper-right corner of the title bar of the text editor screen to minimize.) Next, maximize the browser. (Click on the browser button in the task bar at the bottom of your screen.)

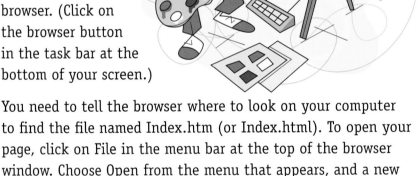

You need to tell the browser where to look on your computer to find the file named Index.htm (or Index.html). To open your page, click on File in the menu bar at the top of the browser window. Choose Open from the menu that appears, and a new screen will come up. Double-click on Browse. You need

TECHNO TIP

Most servers ask that you name your first page (also called a home page) Index.htm or Index.html. That way the server will know which page to show first. You can name the other pages anything you want.

However, it's a good idea to keep the other file names short, too. For example, if your page was about how much you love tuna, you could name it Tuna.htm (or Tuna.html). You could also call it HowILoveTuna.htm, but that takes more time and also leaves a lot of places to make a mistake. This could cause big problems later on!

to tell the computer what drive the file is in. Click on the black arrow next to the Look in: box at the top, and choose 3½ Floppy (A:). Your saved .htm or .html file should be there. Just click OK, and there's your page!

ADDING MORE CONTENT

Now that you know how to save a file, how to open the file in the browser window, and how the basic tags work, you're ready to add more information to your Web page. Minimize the browser window by clicking on the minus button in the title bar, and maximize the editor by clicking in the text editor button on the task bar at the bottom of your screen.

It's time to put that outline you wrote to good use. But what information should you put where? Take a look at your welcome page. When you meet someone new, you introduce yourself, right? Well, it's not much different on the Web. When viewers reach your site, they expect a welcome and an introduction. That way, they'll know what your site is all about.

Check out your outline's categories and subcategories. Now think of how you want them to be worded on the Web page. They should be short so people can read them quickly. However, they should also be entertaining. Write it all down on a piece of paper, and get ready to type it into code.

Type your new content into your text editor. Remember, the information should go beneath the **<BODY>** tag after the closing heading tag **</H1>**. Press enter to go down a space after the heading. This will make your code neater and easier to read. For example, your page might now look like this:

<HTML>

<HEAD>

<TITLE>Welcome**</TITLE>**

</HEAD>

<BODY>

<H1>Welcome to My Web Page, Cyber Dudes**</H1>**

This is a personal Web page that belongs to your host, Nettie Master. To find out more about marvelous me, give the links below a little bite with your mouse, and you'll begin your journey into Master Mania.

The Family Tree

This page is devoted to my fun family.

It includes some weird moments they forgave me for.

It includes some caught-in-action photos.

My Cool Friends

I have some unbelievably cool comrades.

Check out their senses of humor.

They're in some of my best artwork.

What's up With Me!

Meet my dog Elvis.

Check out my awesome music.

I have some favorite hobbies you might like, too!

</BODY>

</HTML>

Check to make sure that you have typed all the information after the opening **<BODY>** tag and before the closing **</BODY>** tag. Make sure that the closing **</HTML>** tag is still the last line on the page.

It's always a good idea to go back and check your spelling and punctuation once you finish typing. It's especially important on the Web. Everything you put on the Web can be seen by millions of people. Mistakes can make it look like you're not so smart.

Go ahead and save your work again. This time click on File from the menu bar, and then click on Save, not Save As. You have already saved the file as Index.htm (or Index.html), and the computer remembers that. All you have to do now is tell the computer to save the new information. It knows where and how to save it. Cool, huh?

A REFRESHING CHANGE

Now that your changes are saved to the disk, it's time to open the browser again. Minimize your text editor by clicking on the minus box in the title bar. Now maximize the browser from the button on the bottom task bar.

You probably see that nothing on your Web page has changed. That's OK—it should look that way. You saved the file on your

TECHNO TIP

Oh, the embarrassment of a misspelled word. On the Web, it's the same as meeting a cool new person...and having broccoli in between your front teeth! *Always check your work!*

floppy disk, but you haven't told the browser about the changes yet. You have to refresh the page to do that.

Click on the Refresh (or Reload) button from the tool bar at the top of the browser screen, and—presto!—your Web page changes. Now *that's* refreshing! (For the AOL browser, you need to right click your mouse and then choose Refresh from the menu that shows up.)

But wait a minute! All of your information is on the page, but it looks terrible. It's all squished together. That doesn't look anything like how you typed it. It's time to learn the codes that will help you format your page. Format is when you set something up so it looks a certain way.

Fantastic Formatting

You will need to give your page some spacing. Now's a good time to learn a new tag—the paragraph tag. Just put it in before and after the text where you want to create a little space. Like most HTML tags, the paragraph tag has an opening tag **(<P>)** and a closing tag **(</P>)**. If you put the paragraph tags in the sample page, it would look like:

<H1>Welcome to My Web Page, Cyber Dudes**</H1>**

<P>Welcome to my page. This is a personal Web page that belongs to your host, Nettie Master. To find out more about marvelous me, give the links below a little bite with your mouse, and you'll begin your journey into Master Mania. **</P>**

<P>The Family Tree

This page is devoted to my fun family.

It tells about some weird moments they forgave me for.

It has some caught-in-action photos.

My Cool Friends

I have some unbelievably cool comrades.

Check out our crazy sense of humor.

They're in some of my best artwork.

What's up With Me!

Meet my dog Elvis.

Check out my awesome music.

I have some favorite hobbies you might like, too!**</P>**

</BODY>

</HTML>

WARNING! WARNING! DISK DANGER! DISK DANGER!

Avoid doom: Never take out a disk that you are working on. If the light on the disk drive is on, leave the disk in. If you take it out, you'll have a Cyber Crash! Your computer might freeze up, and you'll have to restart it. You might even hurt the computer or the disk. Worst of all, you'll lose all of your unsaved work. If your floppy disk has been damaged, you may also lose any saved work. Yikes!

OK, you've put the **<P>** tags around the welcome information at the top and around the category section. Why don't you check to see how the page looks now? First, you have to save your file again. Click on File at the top of the screen, and then choose Save.

Now it's time to tell the browser about the changes. Minimize your editor (with the minus box in the upper-right corner of the title bar), and maximize your browser (with the browser button on the task bar at the bottom of your screen).

Do you remember the next step? You need to tell the browser that changes have been made. Click on the Refresh (or Reload) button at the top of the screen. You'll see that there's now a space after the introduction. That's better, but wouldn't the page look nicer with some space between the categories?

One way you can do this is to use the line break tag **(<BR>)**. The **
** tag makes a line break that's a smaller space than the **<P>** tag. It's perfect for when you want to put one line of text below another. And here's good news: The **
** tag does not need a closing tag, so you don't have to worry about that at all.

Minimize the browser (with the minus box in the title bar). Open up your editor by clicking on the editor button on the task bar.

Now put the **
** tag between the categories to clean up the page a little. Type the tag at the end of each line in the categories. (You don't need one on the last line.) While you're at it, why don't you add a set of **<P>** tags around each of the categories? That should help the spacing problems!

<HTML>

<BODY>

<H1>Welcome to My Web**</H1>**

<P>Welcome to my page. This is a personal Web page that belongs to your host, Nettie Master. To find out more about marvelous me, give the links below a little bite with your mouse, and you'll begin your journey into Master Mania.**</P>**

<P>The Family Tree**
**

This page is devoted to my fun family.**
**

It tells about some weird moments they forgave me for.**
**

It has some caught-in-the-action photos.**</P>**

<P>My Cool Friends**
**

I have some unbelievably cool comrades.**
**

Check out our crazy sense of humor.**
**

They're in some of my best artwork.**</P>**

<P>What's up With Me!**
**

Meet my dog Elvis.**
**

Check out my awesome music.**
**

You can find out about some of my favorite hobbies.**</P>**

</BODY>

</HTML>

Check to make sure your brackets are going the right way and that you have opening **<P>** tags and closing **</P>** tags. Remember, you don't need a closing tag for the **
** tag.

Time for another checkup! Let's see how the page looks now. Click File and Save, and then minimize the editor. Maximize your browser, and click the Refresh (or Reload) button. (If you don't remember how to maximize and minimize, look back at page 32.)

Wow! It's starting to look like a real Web page. Those **
** and **<P>** tags make a big difference!

Now You're Stylin'

The page is beginning to take shape! It's time to add some flavor to your text. Normal text just sits on a page waiting to be read. But have you ever noticed how sometimes the text can just grab your attention? Now that's the way to get noticed. Let's make your text stand up and shout.

TECHNO TIP

Did you notice that the page is a bit different? The words have changed a little. A lot of times, you might want to reword some things as you're working on your page. Go for it! Always be ready to change things or add cool new ideas to your page as you think of them. That's how you make a Web page great.

There are many styles that will help your text stand out. Below are some of the most common. Notice each has an opening tag and a closing tag. The tags go around the word or words that you want to change.

Bold **<B>**This makes the text bold, or heavier and darker.**</B>**

Italic **<I>**This makes the text italic, which means the type leans.**</I>**

Underline **<U>**This underlines all of the text between the tags.**</U>**

~~Strike~~ **<STRIKE>**This puts a line through the middle of the text.**</STRIKE>**

Blink **<BLINK>**This makes the text blink on and off.**</BLINK>**

Super^{script} **^{**This raises the text that is in the tags.**}** (For example, you would use this with a word like 3rd. The code for that would look like 3**^{**rd**}**.)

Sub$_{script}$ **_{**This lowers the text that is in the tags.**}** (You would use this one on words like H_2O. The code would look like H**_{**2**}**O.)

You can use more than one style at the same time. This is when nesting is important. Remember that with nesting, one set of tags must go completely inside of the other set of tags. Look, for example, at a sentence like this:

<B><I>This text will now be bold and italic.**</I></B>**

You can see that this sentence started off by changing the text to bold with the **<B>** tag. Since this tag was opened first, it must be closed last. The opening **<I>** and the closing **</I>** tags change this text to bold and italic. Since it came second, the italic tags must be nested between the **<B>** and the **</B>**.

Experiment with the different types of text styles. You don't want to use them too much, though. Too many styles can boggle the mind. You want your viewer to look around your site, not look around for some aspirin to get rid of a headache from looking at too many styles!

Adding Some Color

Web pages can look OK without color, but just a little bit of color can really add a whole new dimension to your page. It makes the Web page more eye-catching and more exciting for viewers to look at. In other words, it helps make your page cool!

One of the easiest ways to add color to the page is to put in a color background. The **attribute** used is **BGCOLOR**, which stands for background color. The **BGCOLOR** attributes are included inside the body tags. All you have to do is type the color you want in quotation marks. It'll look something like this:

> **WEB WORDS**
> An **attribute** helps further describe what a tag will look like. It tells the computer more specific information. It describes the tag.

<BODY BGCOLOR="color name">

Since BGCOLOR is an attribute, it doesn't need a closing tag. It just stays right there, snuggled up next to the **<BODY>** tag.

But before you go trying to tell the computer some fancy colors like lavender or burgundy, you should know that

> **SAY WHAT?**
> You certainly know a lot of the 16 colors recognized by your computer, such as blue, green, and yellow. But some of those other names are pretty funky. For example, maroon is a deep purplish color. Magenta is another weird-sounding word. It's actually a very bright cross between purple and red. It looks a little like hot pink. And what's with that cyan word? You've probably never even *heard* of that one! Cyan is a mixture of blue and green.

computers only know the exact names for 16 colors. These colors are

If you type the word for any other color besides these, you will only confuse the computer. So, if you want a yellow background, you would type:

<BODY BGCOLOR="yellow">

But wait! What if you do want a fancier color like lavender or burgundy? Are you stuck with just those 16 colors? Not to worry! There are lots of other choices for colors on the Web. It's just a little more confusing to tell the computer what color you want. You do it with hexadecimals (hek-zuh-DE-si-muhls).

The hexadecimals system is a mathematical way of telling the computer what color you want. Hexadecimals are six-digit numbers. The first two digits show how much red will be in the color. The second two digits show how much green will be in the color. The last two digits show how much blue there will be.

It's a little like mixing paint colors. The computer virtually mixes all of these colors together to come up with a new shade. You just have to tell the computer how much of each to add.

You do this through what letters or numbers you put in the digits. The hexadecimals system uses the numbers 0, 3, 6, and 9, and the letters C and F. The 0 is the darkest of that color, and the F is the lightest of that color. So if you put a 00 in the first two digits of the number, that would add the darkest red there is to the new color that you are making. You can combine the letters and numbers together in any way you want. In fact, there are so many combinations in this system that you can make millions of different colors with it!

Play around making your own colors. Just follow the information in the following chart to remember how to go darker and lighter.

Darker				Lighter	
0	3	6	9	C	F

You can then put that new color in the code as you did the names of colors earlier. You just have to put a number sign (#) before the hexadecimal. The code should look like this:

<BODY BGCOLOR="#FF3399">

This would give you a nice, hot pink background on your page. But don't forget your design tips! This color might be cool to look at, but it would be very hard for your viewers to read. Play around with the numbers to see what might work a little bit better. You should try going a little bit darker to make it easier on your viewers' eyes. Keep saving your work and refreshing it in the browser to see how the different backgrounds look.

Don't worry if you're still a little confused by the hexadecimals system. It's a hard one! There's more information on

TECHNO TIPS

Not all browsers were created equal. Because browsers are made by different companies, they're all a little bit different. Some things may not look exactly the same on each browser. Colors are one of those things. What may be a light blue in one browser can turn out to be a green in another. It just depends on the way the browser is programmed to display it. There's really nothing you can do to control it.

hexadecimals (including a chart with some sample colors) in Chapter 7.

What Are Fonts?

A font is a type of lettering or different-styled text. You can see many examples of fonts or typefaces by looking on your own computer. Look under Edit in your text editor on the file menu bar. Select Font or Set Font, and you will see a variety of fonts, each with its own name. Try selecting one and typing in a few words to see what it looks like. Some common fonts found on most computers are Garamond, Arial, Times New Roman, and Helvetica.

The problem with choosing typefaces or fonts for your page comes when you add some of the fun types you find, like Fajita or Jokerman. These fonts may be on your computer but won't necessarily be on your viewers' computers. If their computers don't have the font you used, the computers will substitute it with a general one that it does have. There goes all the ultra-cool-looking text you planned! That's why it's a good idea to use a common font that most computers have, such as those listed above. You can then jazz up the font with color and size.

TECHNO TIPS

To have a little more fun and to learn more about what you're doing, try experimenting with the **SIZE**, **FACE,** and **COLOR** attributes by adding them to your code. Be sure to save and refresh the page to view your changes.

To change the text on your page, you'll use the **<FONT>** tag with the text, followed by the closing **</FONT>** tag. The **<FONT>** tag has several attributes, too: **FACE, SIZE,** and **COLOR.** Just like the attributes you've learned earlier, these should be surrounded by quotation marks and in brackets. They are used to explain to the browser exactly what you want to do with the **<FONT>** tag. The **FACE** attribute tells the browser the name of the font you will use. The **SIZE** attribute shows how big you want your text to be. The **COLOR** attribute tells which color you want the text to be.

FONTS ARE OUR FRIENDS

The **<FONT>** tag can be used to change a large section of text, a sentence, or even just one word. You will place the opening tag before the text you want to change the look of and the closing tag directly after. Include the **FACE** attribute to the **<FONT>** tag to tell the browser you want to change the typeface.

<FONT FACE="Garamond">Now any text that appears here will be in Garamond typeface until you put in the closing tag.**</FONT>**

The **SIZE** attribute of the **<FONT>** tag is used to set how big you want your text to be. The smallest number on this scale is 1.

<FONT FACE="Garamond" SIZE="3">Now you have a typeface set in Garamond with a type size of 3.**</FONT>**

All that you've learned about color will come in handy now, because **COLOR** is an attribute of the **<FONT>** tag, too. You can use one of the 16 predetermined colors or a hexadecimal number.

<FONT FACE="Garamond" SIZE="3" COLOR="#FF3369">You should see a Garamond typeface with a type size of 3 in a shade of red.**</FONT>**

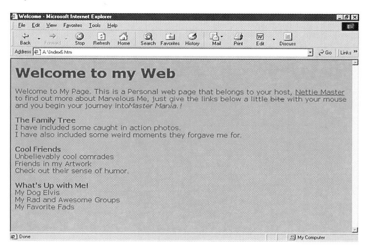

Biting the Bullet

Sometimes you have to give a list of information. It makes it easier for the reader if you put the information in a bulleted list. Bulleted lists have a symbol to the left of the words. Each item is also on a new line. Bulleted lists are great because they

- are easy to read.
- break out the important information.
- look nice in the page design.

You can make bullets on your Web page, too. The tags used for bullets are called lists. There are two types of lists for you to use. There are unordered lists **<UL>** and ordered lists **<OL>**. The tags for an unordered, or bulleted, list looks like this:

<UL> The opening unordered list tag

<LI> The first bulleted text

<LI> The second bulleted text

<LI> The third bulleted text

</UL> The closing unordered list tag

If you want a numbered list, you use the ordered list tags. They work a lot like the unordered list tags, but the opening tag is **<OL>** and the closing tag is **</OL>**. The **<LI>** tag is still the same. The list will start with 1 and go up from there. For example, if the code was

<OL>

<LI> This is an example of an ordered list.

<LI> It uses numbers to head the items in the list.

<LI> The numbers are listed in order.

</OL>

It would look like this:

1. This is an example of an ordered list.

2. It uses numbers to head the items in the list.

3. The numbers are listed in order.

The Home Rule

Sometimes you want to divide sections of text, or you want to separate some pictures. That's when you add a home rule. You can use a home rule to divide things on your page. Rule is just another word for line. Basically, you are adding a line to split things up. The home rule has an opening tag (**<HR>**) but no closing tag.

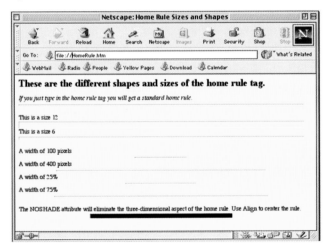

You can adjust the size of the rule. You do this with attributes. Attributes give information about the feature of an object. For example, a line's thickness is an attribute. Its length is one, too. You just type right after the **<HR>** tag any attributes you want. Special attributes of the **<HR>** tag include

- **SIZE**: how thick or thin you want your line to be
- **WIDTH**: how wide you want the line across the window
- **ALIGN**: where you want the line—left, right, or center
- **COLOR**: what color you want the line to be

- **NOSHADE:** if you want the line to be flat instead of 3-D (if you don't mark this, all home rules pop out in 3-D)

Here are some examples of home rule codes. Notice how the attributes have an equal sign after them. Any information you tell the computer about the attributes should be after an equal sign and in quotation marks.

<HR>[SIZE="2" WIDTH="50%" ALIGN="center">

<HR>[SIZE="8" WIDTH="50%" ALIGN="center">

Did you see how the size of a line is measured by a number, but the width is measured by a percentage? It's easier to use a percentage for the width. You just have to decide how far across the window you want the line to go. If you want it to go halfway, that would be 50%. If you want it to go more, you could make it something like 70%. If you want it to go less, you could put 35%.

A TIME TO LINK

Part of what makes Web pages fun is that you can link them together. These are called hyperlinks. Hyperlinks are what have made the Web such a popular place. Hyperlinks let you jump from one spot on a page to another spot on the same page and to jump from one page to another page with the simple click of a mouse!

So how does this work? For hyperlinks, you use tags called anchors. These anchors are super-easy, so they're a quick and cool thing to add to your page. The opening anchor tag is **<A>**, and the closing anchor tag is **</A>**.

There are two types of anchor tags: One set of anchor tags

MEMORY CHECK

Just a friendly reminder with these new tags: If you open it, close it. Once you have the opening tag typed in, don't forget to add the closing tag. The computer will get really confused if you don't.

lets you link a word or sentence at the top of your page to a place at the bottom of your page. The other type of anchor tag links pages together. This means you can let the viewer easily jump to another page on your site. Most welcome pages have links to all of the site's other pages.

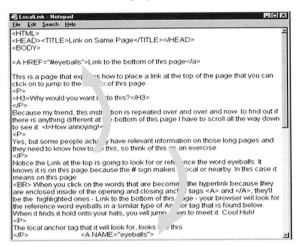

The first type of hyperlink is good for long pages that have lots of information. The reader doesn't have to scroll through a lot of junk to get to another part of the page. For example, sometimes Web pages will have a bulleted list of subjects at the top. The rest of the page is filled with information about those subjects. The Web designer makes the words in the bulleted list link so people can jump straight to the subject they want. Otherwise, they would have to hunt around to find what they need. No one likes to do that!

When you make a hyperlink like this, you need to find a way to tell the computer where it should jump to. That's where the anchor tag comes in. You put an attribute with the anchor tag that tells the computer where to go. That attribute is the **H**yperlink **Ref**erence. It's shortened to **HREF** in the code. For example, if you wanted the computer to jump to the word "Eyeballs" from a link, you would type

<A HREF="#Eyeballs">

The quotation marks ("") and the number sign (#) tell the computer that this is the link it should look for. (And don't forget that you have to put that closing bracket at the end of the line.)

A hyperlink is always highlighted on a Web page. It's usually underlined and a different color. To make that link show up on the page, you have to write that into the code. You have probably seen the words "Click here" highlighted on a Web page. Go ahead and use that on your Web page, too. The words "Click here" will go right after the end of the Eyeballs code and before the closing tag for the anchor (**</A>**). Your code will look like this:

<A HREF="#Eyeballs">Click here**</A>**

"Click here" is now highlighted on the Web page. Viewers will know that it is a link.

But the anchor doesn't end there. You have to put in a second anchor tag to tell the computer where to land. The first anchor actually targets the second anchor. The first set is like a bow and arrow, and the second set is the bull's-eye.

The second set of tags will look the same, but the attribute will be different. The last one was **HREF** because it was the **H**yperlink **Ref**erence. This second set names the **HREF** so it's called **NAME**. A **NAME** tag can be placed anywhere within the opening and closing **<BODY>** tags. It looks like this:

<A NAME="Eyeballs">

There is no closing tag.

LINKIN' UP

OK, now you know how to hop around your page. Let's hop a little farther into the rest of the site. You have ideas on your welcome page that could become pages all by themselves. Then you'd have your very own Web site with lots of pages—all about you! How cool would that be?

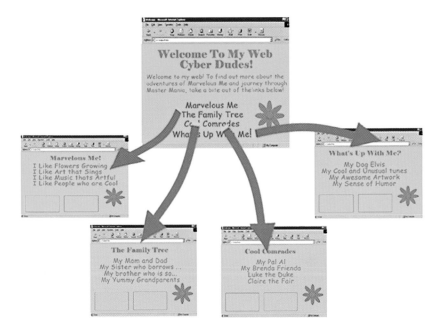

What sort of pages could you create from the sample outline? You could easily do three more. The page you are working on is the welcome page. You could add a second page with The Family Tree. It could be all about your great family. A third page could be from My Cool Friends. It would talk about your friends. The fourth page could be the What's up With Me? section. You can tell people all about your hobbies and your life.

Using the information that you have learned about HTML, open a new file in your editor, and type in the information for the first new page. You can add all of the fun styles and designs that you just learned.

Then you need to save the information in a brand-new file on your floppy disk. Click on File and then Save As like you did when you first saved the Index.htm file. Follow the same steps as last time (see page 40), but this time save the file as Family.htm (or Family.html). Every page that you create must be saved as a separate file with a different name.

When you have saved Family.htm and viewed it in the browser, do the same for the next two pages. Name them Friends.htm (or Friends.html) and Activity.htm (or Activity.html). And now—finally—you're ready to link your pages together.

HERE A LINK, THERE A LINK

You can view each of your pages one at a time in your browser. But instead of having to open each one separately, you can link them together and open them all at once. To do this, you need to use the second type of anchor tag. These anchor tags are used more often because they're how Web sites link all of their pages together. To link your pages, you need to put anchor tags on all of them.

The anchor tags are just like the **HREF** tags that you just learned. Only these tags don't go to a word on the same page. They go to a whole other page. To jump to a new page, you put the page's file name inside the anchor tag as the hyperlink reference (the **HREF** part of the tag). You then have to create a hyperlink on the page so viewers will know where to click to follow the link. Last but not least, you need to add a closing anchor tag.

First, open the welcome page in your editor. Maximize the editor, and click on File and then Open. Choose Index.htm. Put your cursor between the welcome introduction paragraph and your first outline category. Go ahead and put the first anchor tag there. The code should look like this:

```
<A HREF="Family.htm">The Family Tree</A>
```

Add the rest of the anchor tags just above their categories. The codes should look like this:

```
<A HREF="Friends.htm">My Cool Friends</A>
```

```
<A HREF="Activity.htm">What's up With Me?</A>
```

Don't forget that if you have saved your files with .html at the end (such as Index.html), you should put that "l" in your attribute, too.

Now you have created a hyperlink from your welcome page to the rest of the pages. Save the Index.htm file, and minimize your text editor. Maximize the browser. Open the Index.htm file in your browser, and you will see that the links are now highlighted. Click on any of the links to go to another page on your site.

You're not done linking yet, though. You haven't linked any of the pages back to the Welcome page. Minimize your browser, and maximize the text editor. Open up The Family Tree page to start making a hyperlink back to the Welcome page.

You need to make an anchor tag with a reference back to Index.htm. It's pretty much just like you did before. Only this time, you will make the words "Go back to the welcome page" a highlighted link. Type in this code on your page where you want the hyperlink to appear:

<A HREF="Index.htm">Go back to the welcome page**</A>**

Save your file, and open it in the browser. Then check to see if the link works. It should take you right back to the welcome page. Click on the family page link from the welcome page, and you should return to the family page.

When you are happy with your links, open the next .htm file in the editor, and do the same thing again. Just type in that exact code wherever you want the link to show up. Repeat this with all of your files until you are all linked up and ready to go.

Don't Forget the Autograph!

You've worked *hard* on this Web page. It's time to give yourself a little pat on the back. You deserve some applause for your efforts. After all, you have created these pages. It's only right that you autograph your work.

HTML has just the tag for this—the **<ADDRESS>** tag. Put the address tag just before the closing **</BODY>** tag at the bottom of the page. Don't forget the closing tag (**</ADDRESS>**). Your code will look like this:

> **<ADDRESS>**This page was designed
> by Marvelous Me!**</ADDRESS>**

This code will *align* the autograph to the left side of the page. That is, it will begin at the left side of the page. It would probably look better if you centered it. You just need to add a **<CENTER>** tag to the address tag, like this:

> **<ADDRESS><CENTER>**This page was cleverly designed by the
> marvelous Nettie Master!**</CENTER></ADDRESS>**

You've made it to the end, you've signed your work, and your Web site is finished. Or is it? In the next chapter, you'll learn some fun things you can add to your site to make it even more creative and cool!

Web Site Extras

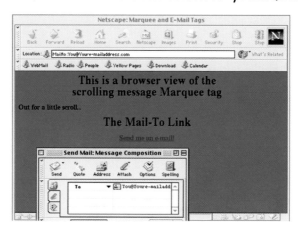

OW THAT YOU have completed a basic page, it's time to add some cool features that make your page both fun and useful. In other words, it's time to get interactive!

A Game of Tags

There are lots of cool tags that will add fun touches to your Web page. Some of them help the viewers interact with you more. Others just look really cool. Best of all, though, is that they're all pretty easy to do!

THE SCROLLING MARQUEE TAG

A marquee (mar-KEE) is the sign outside a theater. It's supposed to get the attention of people as they pass by. HTML has a **<MARQUEE>** tag that is also supposed to get people's attention. It scrolls the text across the screen over and over. It's great animated fun! Just put what you want to say between the opening and closing tags. For example:

<MARQUEE>Out for a little scroll...**</MARQUEE>**

THE MAILTO: LINK TAG

Don't you want to know what your viewers think about your page? The mailto: link tag lets you find out. This is a link that you can create on the page. Viewers click on it, and an e-mail form pops up on their screens. They can then e-mail you directly from your Web site. The mailto: link code can be put in wherever you want the link to be on the page. It shows up as a highlighted hyperlink, so you need to use the anchor tag. The **HREF** part is **"Mailto:"** plus your e-mail address. Whatever you type after the next angle bracket will show up onscreen as the highlighted link. Don't forget to end with the closing anchor tag (**</A>**). The code should look like this:

<A HREF="Mailto:You@Youre-mailaddress.com">
Send me an e-mail!</A>

Cool, isn't it? Just think—all of your viewers can write and tell you what they think about your Web site. And it's a great way to make more e-pals!

Forming an Interactive Page

Getting an e-mail from your page users is great, but what if you want to ask them certain questions? What if, say, you really wanted to find out about their favorite books? Then you would need to add a form to your page. Forms come in lots of shapes and sizes, but they all do the same thing. They let you ask view-

CYBER SAFETY ALERT

A lot of people use their name in e-mail addresses, such as nettie_master@acme.com. This is fine, but it can let people you don't know find out your full name. Create an e-mail that has a made-up or creative online name, such as LuvTheWeb@acme.com. This will help protect your identity.

Also, it's OK to put your e-mail address on your page, but don't put your street address or phone number. Remember, everyone in the world is part of your audience. (See Chapter 1 for any questions about Internet safety.)

ers questions that they can answer right there online. Their answers are then sent to you by e-mail.

When you sign up to go to school or to take a special class, either you or your parents need to fill out a form. This tells the school something about you, such as your name, address, and phone number. The form may also ask your age and other facts about you to make sure you get in the right class. Forms on the Internet do the same thing. They get information about a viewer and then use it to help him or her.

Most forms are made up of text boxes. These boxes can be a rectangle or a square. The viewers type their answers in the text boxes. With just the click of the Submit button, viewers can then send their responses to you by e-mail.

To make a form on your page, you simply use the **<FORM>** tag. (The closing tag is **</FORM>**.) Alone, the form doesn't exactly dance. Add an attribute, though, and that form does a nice little cha-cha for you.

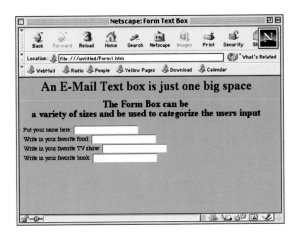

The first attribute is **ACTION**. You'll use this and the mailto: tag to tell the computer that you want the form answers sent to your e-mail address. The **METHOD** attribute tells the browser to actually go on and send the e-mail. The code should look something like this:

<FORM ACTION="mailto:You@Youre-mailaddress.com" METHOD="Post">

Now that the browser knows what the form is supposed to do, it's time to create the text box so the form will appear on the screen. Use the **<INPUT>** tag to create a text box for the information.

Of course, there are also attributes for the **<INPUT>** tag. The **TYPE** attribute tells the browser the type of box you want to make. Because you want to create a text box, you should type in **TYPE="text"**. (Did you notice that the type of the box is in quotation marks? Remember, you have to put quotation marks around what you want to tell the computer about an attribute.) The **NAME** attribute will remind you what question the viewers are answering. The **SIZE** attribute tells the computer how many letters or numbers wide you want the box to be. Put it all together, and the code looks like this:

<INPUT TYPE="text" NAME="book character" SIZE="30">Who is your favorite book character?

Create as many of these boxes as you have questions. They can be in lots of sizes. You don't have to use just one size.

It's nice to have the questions on your site, but don't forget to add a **<BUTTON>** tag. Otherwise, the viewers don't have any way to send you their answers. It's not much good to fill out a form that you can't send in! Use the **<BUTTON>** tag to make a submit button that will send the answers to your e-mail address. You can also use it to make a reset button. That's a good idea in case the viewer makes a mistake and wants to start over. (Don't forget the closing tag when you're typing in your code: **</BUTTON>**.)

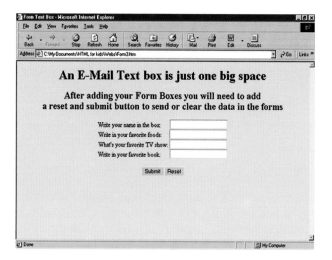

The attributes for the **<BUTTON>** tag include **TYPE** and **VALUE**. The **TYPE** attribute tells what kind of button you are creating. The **VALUE** attribute tells what the button will do. Anything that is between the brackets of the last two tags is the text that will show up on the button. For instance, the submit button code should look like this:

<BUTTON TYPE="Submit" VALUE="Send Data">Submit**</BUTTON>**

You should place the submit button code just after the code for the last text box.

To create the reset button, place this code next to the code for the submit button:

<BUTTON TYPE="Reset" VALUE="Reset Data">Reset</BUTTON>

Now you are ready to close your form. Just add the closing **</FORM>** tag, and you are done!

Your form boxes will automatically align to the left. If they are different sizes, and you want them to look neater, put them in a table. Use the **<TABLE>** tag to do this. You also need to use the **<TR>** and **<TD>** tags. The **<TR>** tag opens and closes (**</TR>**) each table row. The **<TD>** tag shows what data will be in the table. In other words, it tells how many columns are in the table. Start off with the opening **<TABLE>** tag, and then start the first row with a **<TR>** tag. Then, just include each **<INPUT>** tag inside of **<TD>** and **</TD>** tags like this:

```
<FORM ACTION="mailto:You@Youre-mailaddress.com"
              METHOD="Post">

<TABLE ALIGN="center">
<TR>
<TD>Place your name here:<INPUT TYPE="text" NAME="name"
SIZE="30"></TD>
<TD>Place your hometown here:<INPUT TYPE="text"
NAME="hometown" SIZE="30"></TD>
<TD>Place your favorite sports team here:<INPUT TYPE="text"
NAME="sports team" SIZE="30"></TD>
<TD><BUTTON TYPE="Submit" VALUE="Send
Data">Submit</BUTTON></TD>
<TD><BUTTON TYPE="Reset" VALUE="Reset
Data">Reset</BUTTON></TD>
</TR>
</TABLE>
</FORM>
```

Fancying up the Forms

Go ahead and save your work, and then look at the form in the browser. The online form makes the page pretty fun, doesn't it? But it's also sort of plain right now. You can make the design of the form even cooler.

For example, you can ask a question and then give viewers some answers to choose from. The viewers can mark off their answers with checkboxes or radio buttons. It's like an online multiple-choice question! Checkboxes are small square boxes that viewers can click on to show their choices. A checkmark will show up in the box when viewers click there. A radio button is a small circle that is used for the same thing. A black dot appears in a radio button when viewers click in it.

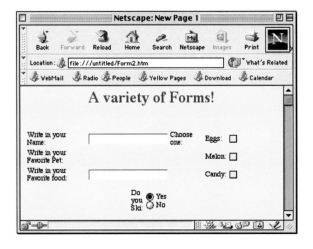

You tell the computer which type of button you want by using the **TYPE** attribute of the **<INPUT>** tag. The tag has a **NAME** attribute. **NAME** shows what the group of buttons is for. You use the **VALUE** attribute to show the computer what that one button is for. The code for radio buttons would look like this:

<HTML>
<BODY>
What is your favorite ice cream flavor?
<FORM ACTION="mailto:You@Youre-mailaddress.com"

```
                METHOD="Post">
    <INPUT TYPE="Radio" NAME="Ice Cream"
        Value="Chocolate">Chocolate
    <INPUT TYPE="Radio" NAME="Ice Cream"
        Value="Strawberry">Strawberry
    <INPUT TYPE="Radio" NAME="Ice Cream"
        Value="Vanilla">Vanilla
    <INPUT TYPE="Submit" VALUE="Send Data">
                </FORM>
                </BODY>
                </HTML>
```

If you want to use squares instead of circles, you just tell the computer to use checkboxes instead of radio buttons. Put **TYPE="Checkbox"** instead of **TYPE="Radio"**.

```
    <INPUT TYPE="Checkbox" NAME="Ice Cream"
        Value="Lemon">Lemon
```

You've Been Framed!

The **<FRAME>** tag is a structure tag that sets up a frame. It divides the page into sections, or "windows." Each section has its own information. There's a place for everything, and everything is in its place.

Building a frame is like building a house. The frame is the support a house is built on. Just like a house can have many rooms, a frame can have many windows that each display information.

The more sections you make in a frame page, the smaller each section has to be. The smaller the section is, the less information you will be able to display nicely. It's important, then, to limit the number of frames on a page.

You can use a frame to set aside a section of your Web page for the title of your Web site. You can also set up a frame in the page for all of the links to the rest of your site.

Building a **<FRAME>** begins with the **<FRAMESET>** tag. This is like the structure of the house. The individual frames that are inside the **<FRAMESET>** tag are like the rooms inside the house. Each frame has a name and shows an .htm file. The **NAME** attribute names the frame so you can use that name later in the code.

```
<FRAMESET>
<FRAME NAME="Top">
<FRAME NAME="Main">
<FRAME NAME="Bottom">
</FRAMESET>
```

The **<FRAMESET>** tag also has a **ROWS** attribute. You tell the computer how many rows there will be by how many numbers you put after the attribute. The numbers are separated by commas. The numbers also tell the computer how tall each row should be. The rows will automatically go all the way across the width of the screen, but you have to tell the computer how tall each one will be. For example, look at the following:

```
<FRAMESET ROWS="50,*,50">
```

This code tells the browser that there will be three rows. The first row will start at the top of the screen and come down 50 **pixels**. The third row is also 50 pixels. It will stretch 50 pixels from the bottom going up.

WEB WORDS

A **pixel** (PIK-suhl) is a unit of measurement for the computer screen. A standard screen is 640 pixels across and 480 pixels down.

You probably noticed that the middle row doesn't have a number. It has a * sign. This is a computer shortcut for saying "all the rest." Since the top row is using the first 50 pixels of the screen and the bottom row is using the last 50 pixels, you want the middle row to use whatever space is left over so there are no empty spots on the screen. You could subtract it out and tell the computer a specific number, but you don't have to! Just give the computer the * symbol, and it will figure it out for you.

You know how to set up the frames now, but you still have to tell the computer what information to put inside the frames. You will need to use the **SRC** attribute, or the source attribute. This tells the computer where to look for the file for that window.

That bottom row would be perfect to put all of the hyperlinks to get to the rest of your site. If you do that, though, you have to add a **TARGET** attribute to your code. The **TARGET** attribute tells the browser in which frame to show a page when a hyperlink is clicked on. If you don't put anything about that, the pages you link to will always come up in the bottom frame. That's a pretty small space, and the viewers would probably have trouble seeing everything.

You want to use the **TARGET** attribute to tell the browser to show that page in the middle frame. In fact, that's the only thing that middle main frame is going to be used for on this page. It's always going to show whatever page the viewer is looking at. It will change each time the viewer clicks on a different link, but the top and bottom frames will always remain the same. Once done, your code will look something like this:

```
<HTML>
<HEAD>
<TITLE>Frameset Page with 3 Frame Rows</TITLE>
</HEAD>
<FRAMESET Rows="50,*,50">
<FRAME NAME="Top" SRC="Heading.htm">
<FRAME NAME="Main" SRC="Welcome.htm">
<FRAME NAME="Bottom" SRC="Navigate.htm"
TARGET="Main">
</FRAMESET>
</HTML>
```

The **SRC** attributes tell the browser to display a page called "Heading.htm" inside the top frame, "Welcome.htm" in the main frame, and "Navigate.htm" in the bottom frame. The **TARGET="Main"** attribute in the bottom frame tells the computer where to send anything that's opened there. This code sends it straight to the bigger main frame.

Also notice that there are no **<BODY>** tags in a frame page. That is because there is nothing to type in the body section for the viewer to see.

Why don't you give this one a whirl? Try creating your own frame page. Open your editor, and type the code in. Change the name of the three file names to three of the ones you have saved on your floppy disk (Family.htm, Friends.htm, and Activity.htm). Then save your file as FramePage.htm. This name will help you remember that this is the page with the frames. Now look at it in the browser.

Frames are fun to play with! Go ahead and goof around with them. For example, you can change the size of the rows. The row size can vary depending on how many pixels you want to use. Fifty pixels is not very much space, but it is big enough for a title at the top of

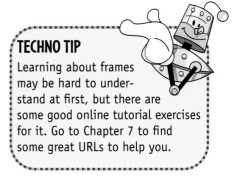

TECHNO TIP

Learning about frames may be hard to understand at first, but there are some good online tutorial exercises for it. Go to Chapter 7 to find some great URLs to help you.

the page or for navigational links at the bottom. Try changing the row sizes to see what that looks like. Save your file, and refresh your browser to see the difference.

Once you understand how the rows work, you can try playing with columns in the **<FRAMESET>** page. The attribute for columns is **COLS**. Just use **COLS** instead of **ROWS** in the code. If you want to use both, you have to create a different **<FRAMESET>** for both the columns and the rows. Make a **<FRAMESET>** for the frame that you want to go all the way across (row) or all the way down (column) first. Then create another **<FRAMESET>** for the rest of the page.

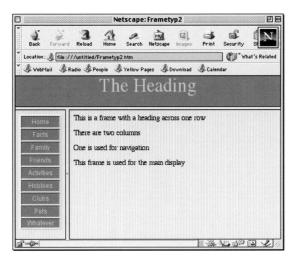

Experiment with rows first. Then if you understand the idea, try adding columns.

Make a Little Noise

Another fun interactive trick is adding sound to your pages. Viewers can rock and roll right along with their surfing! Adding sound requires a few tags and a little knowledge of file extensions. There are sound file extensions: .ram, .Midi, .aif, .au, and .wav. There are more, but those are the most popular. You can find lots of sounds on the Web to download (remember to ask permission from the Webmaster first).

In order for viewers to hear sound on their computers, they must have a sound card installed. They must also have the correct software, which are called plug-ins. Most browsers that are higher than a 4.0 version have a good supply of plug-ins to choose from, so this shouldn't be a problem.

YOU'VE GOT SOUND!

Sounds you find on the Web are cool, but how would you like to make your own sounds for your Web site? If you want to create your own voice recording and you have a microphone on your computer, open your Sound Recorder. It is in the Start menu. Then click on Programs, and click on Accessories. Click on the microphone button on the right, and record. Save this as a .wav file.

On a Macintosh computer, go to the apple menu in the top-left corner. Click on it, and go to Control Panels. Click on Monitors & Sound when the drop-down menu appears. Click on the Sound button. Select Microphone in the Sound Input section. Save your recording as an .aif file.

Since each browser works a little bit differently, you will need to add the same sound tag in two places to make sure that it works for all of your viewers and their browsers. Begin by putting the **<BGSOUND>** tag in the opening **<BODY>** tag. Next, put an **<EMBED>** tag in for other browsers. Remember the old **SRC** attribute? That's the source attribute. You have to tell the browser the name of your sound file and where the browser can find it. The code would look something like this:

```
<BODY BGSOUND SRC="YourGroovySound.wav" LOOP=Infinite>
     <EMBED SRC="YourGroovySound.wav" LOOP=True>
```

The **LOOP** attribute tells the browser how many times you want the sound recording to play. Infinite and True mean that it should play over and over forever. If you type in a number instead, it will play the sound that many times.

Great Jumpin' Java!

Web pages are about way more than just HTML. For example, Java is a complex computer language used to design software programs and Web pages. Visual Basic, Perl, CGI, and ASP are other types of languages that can build Web pages. These are really hard, though, and they would take a lot of studying before you would be able to use them.

However, there is a complex language that you can copy and paste into your own HTML code to make some cool things happen. It's called JavaScript. It's quite different from your usual cup of Java.

The beauty of JavaScript code is that you can copy and paste it from another source to your page. There are many resources on the Web that allow you to do just that. In return, you just have to put a link on your page that goes to their site. But if you don't have a good understanding of where to put the code, it won't work.

There are a few things you need to know before you start copying and pasting. The first thing is that you need to know exactly where to place it.

> **CYBER SAFETY ALERT**
> In Javascript, type everything as you see it, and leave spaces only where you see them. Check your code well for missing elements and spelling. Any small mistake will keep it from working.

JavaScript is called a scripting language because of the way it writes its code. Because of this, it needs to be placed in the head section of your Web page document. This is where the browser will look for the information first.

You also must use the **<SCRIPT>** opening tag and the **</SCRIPT>** closing tag. **LANGUAGE** is an attribute of the **<SCRIPT>** tag, and JavaScript is the type of language that you will use.

The second thing you need to know is that all JavaScript language is written inside of comment tags. Remember how a comment tag lets you write notes to yourself that won't show up on the Web page? JavaScript is completely written inside of the comment tags. It has instructions that your browser has to read but your viewers don't need to see. The comment tag begins with a **<!--** and it ends with a **--//>**. (See page 41 for a refresher on comment tags.)

You should open a JavaScript section like this:

<HEAD>
<TITLE>Title of this page**</TITLE>**

<SCRIPT LANGUAGE="JavaScript">
<!--

Notice that the comment tag above has been opened above using the **<!--**. Everything that follows this is inside of the comment tag until you put in the ending tag, which looks like: **--//>**.

There are often two parts to JavaScript. The first part is written in comment tags because it includes all the instructions for what the second part should do. The second part is put in the **<BODY>** section. It shows the viewer what is happening. This is the action part.

Let's try out the code to add some mouse trails to our pages.

The Mouse Trail Code

A mouse trail is a little spray of images that follows along with your mouse as you move it across the screen. It is a truly cool touch for any Web page!

This code was accessed from the library of www.Javascript.com and created by Marcin Wojtowicz. It was altered just a bit for this book. The image below will give you an idea of how the mouse will look on your page when it is moved. There are smiley faces in this trail, but you can put in just about anything that suits your mood. Just choose one of your favorite images.

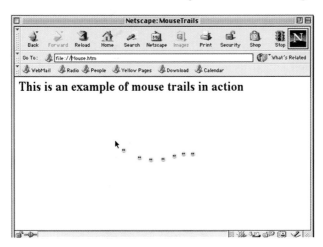

Small images work the best. The image should be 12 pixels wide and 20 pixels high. That's tiny! (The happy face image in this trail is 10 pixels wide by 15 pixels high.) Save the image you choose as Trail.gif.

Now it's time to add the code. Unfortunately, you will have to type in the code from this page, and it is long. Be careful to add all brackets, closing slash marks, and colons. (Not to mention be careful with your spelling.) In this code, the first set of instructions for the browser is put in the **<HEAD>** section, while the second larger portion is put in the **<BODY>** section.

Add this section to the **<HEAD>** section after the closing **</TITLE>** tag. Your code will look like this:

```
<HTML>
<HEAD>
<TITLE>The Mouse Trail Page</TITLE>
<STYLE TYPE="text/css">
BODY {overflow: scroll; overflow-x: hidden;}
</STYLE>
</HEAD>
```

Adding this code to the **<HEAD>** section tells the browser about the way the images will follow the mouse.

Now, insert this code in the **<BODY>** section. You probably won't understand any of this code, but you don't have to! Just carefully type it all in, and you will have a spunky little mouse trail on your Web page. You'll be the envy of all the other plain online rodents! You'll notice that there's a ¶ symbol at the end of the lines. This isn't part of the code, so don't type it in. They're there to show you when you should hit Return to start a new line.

```
<BODY> ¶
<SCRIPT LANGUAGE="JavaScript1.2"> ¶
<!-- Begin ¶
var trailLength = 8 ¶
var path = "Trail.gif" ¶
var isIE = false, isNav = false, range = "all.", style = ".style",
i, d = 0; ¶
var topPix = ".pixelTop", leftPix = ".pixelLeft", images,
storage; ¶
if (document.layers) { ¶
isNav = true, range = "layers.", style = "", topPix = ".top",
leftPix = ".left"; ¶
} else if (document.all) { ¶
isIE = true; ¶
} ¶
function initTrail() { ¶
images = new Array(); ¶
for (i = 0; i < parseInt(trailLength); i++) { ¶
images[i] = new Image(); ¶
images[i].src = path; ¶
} ¶
storage = new Array(); ¶
for (i = 0; i < images.length*3; i++) { ¶
storage[i] = 0; ¶
} ¶
```

```
for (i = 0; i < images.length; i++) { // make divs for IE and
layers for Navigator ¶
(isIE) ? document.write('<div id="obj' + i + '" style="position:
absolute; z-Index: 100; height: 0; width: 0"><img src="' +
images[i].src + '"></div>') : document.write('<layer
name="obj' + i + '" width="0" height="0" z-
index="100"><img src="' + images[i].src + '"></layer>'); ¶
} ¶
trail(); ¶
} ¶
function trail() { ¶
for (i = 0; i < images.length; i++) { ¶
eval("document." + range + "obj" + i + style + topPix + "=" +
storage[d]); ¶
eval("document." + range + "obj" + i + style + leftPix + "=" +
storage[d+1]); ¶
d = d+2; ¶
} ¶
for (i = storage.length; i >= 2; i--) {; ¶
storage[i] = storage[i-2]; ¶
} ¶
d = 0; ¶
clearTimeout(timer); ¶
var timer = setTimeout("trail()", 10); ¶
} ¶
function processEvent(e) {  ¶
if (isIE) { ¶
storage[0] = window.event.y+document.body.scrollTop+10; ¶
storage[1] = window.event.x+document.body.scrollLeft+10; ¶
} else { ¶
storage[0] = e.pageY+12; ¶
storage[1] = e.pageX+12; ¶
} ¶
} ¶
if (isNav) { ¶
```

```
document.captureEvents(Event.MOUSEMOVE); ¶
} ¶
if (isIE || isNav) { ¶
initTrail(); ¶
document.onmousemove = processEvent; ¶
} ¶
// End --> ¶
</SCRIPT> ¶
</BODY> ¶
</HTML> ¶
```

MEMORY CHECK
Don't forget the closing
</SCRIPT>, **</BODY>**,
and **</HTML>** tags!

Phew! You're all done. Save your work, and refresh your browser to see how it looks. If it doesn't work, go back and check your typing. If you still can't get it to work and you can't find your mistake, go to the www.Javascript.com Web site, and copy its version.

Even More Cool Stuff

There's no end to the fun stuff you can add to your page! Codes for all of the below features can be found online. You can easily add them to your page once you get permission from the Webmaster. Check out Chapter 7 for sites that offer code for these features for free!

A PAGE COUNTER

A page counter tallies the number of cyber citizens who have dropped by. You can display it on your first page so viewers will know how many other people have visited.

A GUEST BOOK

You can create a guest book using a simple form. It's a great way to learn more about your viewers. Have your viewers give you specific feedback about themselves or about your page. You can also get fancy and visit one of the sites specializing in guest books that have themes attached. Many of the host providers offer these as part of their services.

Looking Behind the Scenes

With all this HTML and all these extra features, you are well on your way to one very cool Web site! Sometimes when you're out surfing along the Web, though, you'll find the ultimate site. Its coolness just blows you away! It practically has you drooling for a feature that you think is a must-have! And all you can think is,

"How did they do that?" There is a way to find out. It's called View Source.

All you have to do is right-click (or click and hold) on any Web page, and a drop-down menu will appear. Choose View Source (or Page Source), and your text editor will instantly open, displaying the code from that page. (If you can't right-click, select View from the file menu bar, and click on Source or Page Source.) It's like magic!

Chances are there will be more than HTML in there, but you may be able to figure out how to make that feature that you liked so much. You can just cut and paste into the code for your own Web page. Before you go around cutting and pasting, though, remember what you learned in Chapter 1. Be sure to get permission from the Webmaster first.

Sometimes you can't right-click on a Web page because the designers have disabled it. They don't want people to be able to see the codes.

CYBER SAFETY ALERT

Remember that everything on a page is covered by copyright laws. This means you have to ask permission before you can use anything. Many designers are willing to share if you ask, so write to them. If they say no, though, respect the law and don't include it in your page.

Publishing Your Page

So now you've built a really cool Web page. You're all done, right? Whoa! You're not quite done yet. You still have to publish your Web page. A published Web page is any page that you can see on the Web. This book was once just a bunch of papers and drawings, and now you are able to read it. That's because the book was published. Now you have to do the same thing for your Web page: You have to publish it for all to see.

Up until now, you've been saving your text and graphic files on your floppy disk drive. You have been able to see them in the Web browser after you saved and refreshed the page, but that's about it. No one else can see them either. Now is the time to change all that.

Just like this book has a publisher that has put it out for all to see, you need to find a publisher for your Web page. On the Web, though, a publisher is a host server computer. Remember how Chapter 2 talked about how a Web page lives on a host computer? That host computer is like an apartment building that lets you rent space. The company that owns the host server computer lets your page move in and then gives it the support that will help it stand out on the Web.

You give all of the code for your Web site to the host company. It then puts the code on the server computer's hard disk. The server computer holds the Web pages and arranges them while it waits for a viewer to ask to see them. As soon as someone wants to look at the site, the computer reads the pages' codes and sends the information back to the viewer's browser.

How Do You Publish?

First, you need to have your completed Web page. It's time to run through a final checklist to make sure everything works. Go through each and every page, and do these things:

- Run spellcheck. You definitely don't want to be known for a spelling mistake more than you are for how cool your Web page is! Especially not when spellcheck is so easy to use.
- Check to make sure all of your graphics are spelled and typed correctly in the code. You should also make sure that your graphics files are on the floppy disk with the text files. Double-check the code to make sure your file names in there are the same as the files on the disk.

- Check all of the links on the pages. Do they all work? Are there enough to get viewers around on your site easily? Check to make sure your locations are all in the code correctly.
- Check your forms. Testing the forms on your site is easy! When your page first goes online, fill out the information for the form. Press submit, and the information should come to your e-mail. If it doesn't, then something is wrong in your code.
- Check your frames. Make sure that all your links jump to the frame that you want them to.
- Double-check your tags. Make sure you put in opening and closing tags where they're needed. Also check for the equal sign (=) and quotation marks (" ") in the attributes. All you need is one missing mark to mess things up.
- If you have added any other type of language, make sure to check and recheck your code for simple typing and spelling errors.

All of these are very simple things to check. But remember to do it carefully. They may be easy to check, but mistakes can be hard to find. If your page isn't working and you can't find where the problem is, ask a fellow HTML whiz to double-check it for you. Chapter 7 of this book also has a troubleshooting section that will help you find the solutions to common problems.

On Your Mark

Now that you have checked and rechecked your code and everything seems to be working, the next thing to do is test the pages again. You're probably thinking, "What? *Again?!*"

Yes, again. This time, test it on another browser. If you used Netscape Navigator to build your pages, check them in Microsoft Internet Explorer. These are the two most popular browsers. Your viewers could easily be using either one. The problem is each browser has its own way of viewing things, so your page will look different on each. You don't want to risk having your pages look bad to half of your browsers. Not after all your hard work!

Don't worry—the HTML code you learned in this book is standard. That means that both browsers understand it. That doesn't mean, though, that they will show it the same way. By testing the code out in both browsers, you will get a better idea of what will look different on them. For instance, Netscape Navigator makes your page background white if you don't specify a color. Internet Explorer, however, makes the background gray so it looks like you forgot to add a background.

You may need to add some extra code on your page to get around some of the problems. When you test the pages on the other browser, you'll find the problems quickly. And when you see the problems, you'll learn that you have to be more specific about with your attributes. That way, the browser can't get confused at all when it reads them, and you won't have to go back and add extra code to please the browser.

FINDING A HOST PROVIDER

So you've ironed out any bugs with the pages. Now you're ready to hook up to a server computer. But which one should you choose? Chapter 7 lists many free sites where you can put up some pages. Many of the free sites ask you to put a banner ad on your site in return for the free space. That's not too bad a trade.

You should also check out some server computers that you have to pay for. For example, most of the larger Internet Service Providers (ISPs), such as America Online and Earthlink, have spaces where you can put personal Web pages. It's usually included with the monthly fee that you pay the ISP, so it might not cost any more than you're already paying. Usually, though, these pages have really long addresses, which can be a pain.

You might want to consider registering a domain name. A domain name is the site name with its extension (.com, .org, .net, and so on). Only one person can own each domain name, so you first have to check to see if the name you want is already being used by someone else. For example, the VegastheCat.com domain name from Chapter 3 is obviously already taken. Lots of people have the same idea for domain names, so you should be certain to check before you get your heart set on something. (Many host providers will check this for you.)

Once you find a domain name that you want, you just pay a fee (about $17 a year) to "own" the domain name. You can keep that name, then, for as long as you keep paying the fee. No one else can use the domain name while you have it. For example, if you decided to buy a domain name and call it MyCoolWebPage.com, you would first need to check to see if it is still available. If it is, then you can buy it. (You can usually do this through your host provider.)

That doesn't mean you're in the clear once you have a domain name, though. You still have to find a host provider. The provider will put your site on its server and list your domain name as your new Web address:

http://www.MyCoolWebPage.com

If you don't want to mess with a domain name, though, you can just keep the long address that you get from the host provider. You just use the name of the host provider and the member name that it assigns you. Your URL then might look something like this:

http://www.geocities.com/kidszone/happy5278/me.htm

Get Set...

You've found a host provider that you like, and your Web page is good to go. You're all ready to launch. But wait! How exactly do you get your cool Web page from your computer to the host provider's computer? After all, you might be in Ohio, and your host server computer could be in California.

This sounds like a job for FTP, or File Transfer Protocol. FTP is a set of rules that all data must use when it is being transferred over the Internet.

All the information for your Web page is in the files on your floppy disk. Those files need to go from your floppy drive, through your modem, down your telephone wires, back up to the server's telephone lines, and through the server's modem. The server then puts it in your spot on the computer. That's a *long* way to go. You know how sometimes when you have to go a long way you get directions and look at a map to find your way? Well, that's what FTP does for computers. It tells the files how to find their way to the correct computer. It tells them how to pack, what to wear, and where to go.

A few ISPs and host providers (such as AOL) have a built-in method that will automatically put your information in the right FTP mode. If your provider doesn't have that, though, then you need to get the software to do it. If you don't have it on your computer already, you can download a free limited edition from the Web. That should be all you need to get the job done. The program is available at http://www.ipswitch.com.

As soon as you have the program, it's time to connect to your ISP. You should then open your FTP program. You can find it by selecting Start and then Programs on your PC or by selecting the apple and choosing it from the drop-down menu on your Macintosh. An opening screen will appear. Your ISP should have e-mailed you the information you need to log on to the program. The information will include the server's URL, your ID, and your

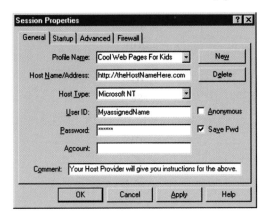

password. Type in a Session Profile Name. That way, the next time you FTP, you can just look for that name. Then all of the information that you just typed in will be there, and you won't have to put it all in again.

Once you have the information filled in, click OK. A new box will come up. It has two sides; one is the local side. That's your connection to your own computer. The other side will connect you to the server computer.

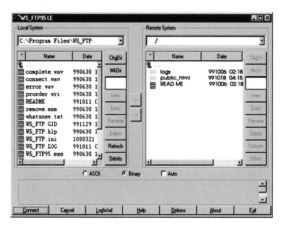

On the Local side, use the scroll bar to go down to the bottom of the list. You will see small blue boxes with a letter next to them. Those letters are the different drives on your computer. Your disk is in the A: drive, so double-click on the letter A. You will see all the files that you created and saved on the disk. They will all have the .htm or .html extension following the name. The graphics files should have either a .gif or .jpg file extension. Sound files will have the .wav extension.

Look just below the two open windows, and you will see three radio buttons. You will use these to tell the program how you want to send your information. You will mostly use the ASCII and Binary formats. The first button is ASCII. Use this when you want to transfer text files (all of your .htm/.html files). Choose the Binary button when you are ready to send the image or sound files.

If you look at the Remote side of the window, you will see a few items listed there. That's the host server's computer. That means you have just connected to your Web site's new space! It's time to start moving the Web pages in and putting its things away. The Remote side has a Public or HTML file folder. Double-click on this to open it. Your Web page is now ready to move in there.

Use the arrows in the middle of the box to highlight all the .htm and .html files. There's an easy way to do this. Click on the first .htm file, and hold down the shift key. Now click the last .htm/.html file, and the computer will know to highlight them all. (You can't do this little shortcut if there are .jpg, .gif, or .wav files mixed in with the .htm and .html ones. If they are all mixed together, just choose the .htm or .html files one by one, and click the arrow to send them over to the Remote side.)

After you have highlighted the files, click on the arrow that points toward the Remote side. The files are then transferred to the host server and put in your personal Web space.

TECHNO TIPS

Not all host providers want you to put your files in the Public or HTML file folder. They might call the folder something else. They'll tell you where to put your files when they e-mail you the directions.

Now go back and highlight the image and sound files by clicking on them. (Don't forget that you need to use the binary option for these files.) Click the same arrow that points toward the Remote side, and the files will be transferred just like the other ones.

When you have transferred all the files to the server, click Exit. Congratulations! You have moved your Web site to the world!

Sometimes there's a short delay until you can see your page on the Web. But this isn't usually the case, so why don't you go online and check out your page? Type your new URL in your browser's address box, and you should see your Web site live. Now you are truly a Webmaster of one very cool Web page!

Don't panic, though, if something has gone wrong and you can't see your page. First, double-check the FTP directions e-mailed to you by your host provider, and make sure you did each step correctly. It's easy to make a mistake there. For example, the provider may have requested that your first page be named Index.htm or Default.html. The provider may also have requested that you put your information in a certain folder. Generally, this folder should appear on the Remote side when you log on.

If you still have problems, you can check with the help desk of your host provider. You can also look on the provider's Web site. The sites sometimes have a list of the step-by-step FTP instructions.

USING AN AUTOMATIC UPLOAD

As mentioned earlier, there are also host providers (such as AOL) that have their own FTP services built right in. They do all of the thinking for you.

For example, to transfer your pages to AOL, you need to go to keyword "My FTP" on AOL's home page. A screen example will pop up. Click on See My FTP Space. A box will then appear and connect you to the remote server.

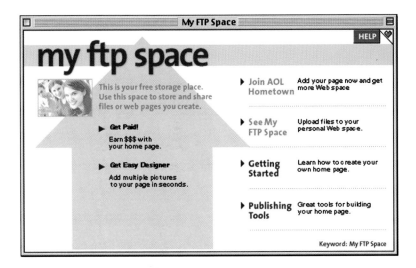

There will be many icons on the bottom of the pop-up screen. Click on the Upload icon. Another box will appear and ask you for your local drive. Just type in A. (Don't use a colon or a back slash, or you will get an error message.)

Next click on Continue. A box with two icons will appear. You now need to retrieve your files, but first you need to tell the computer where to find them. Click on the Select File icon, and a gray Attach File box will appear. Click on the down arrow on the right side of the Look in: box, and choose the A: drive. The A: drive box will appear. You should click on the file you want to upload (Index.htm) and then click on Open. You will see your file listed in the Upload File box. Click the Send icon. If everything worked OK, a small pop-up box will come up to tell you the file transfer was completed. Click on OK to close this box. Now do the rest of the files the same way.

Your site will now officially be on the AOL site. Go to http://members.aol.com/yourscreennamehere/index.htm to check it out.

Geocities also has an automatic upload, and it's a lot like the AOL process. You first must register with Geocities, and the company will assign you a member name at http://www.geocities.com. Once you have this, you can transfer your files using the built-in transfer system. The system is called EZ Upload. And just like the name says, it is very easy to use. (However, you need to have

Netscape Navigator 2.0 or higher or Internet Explorer 3.02 or higher to use EZ Upload.)

Start by going to the Geocities site and clicking on File Manager. Scroll down to the EZ Upload utility, and click on Browse. A box will open up. You need to choose the A: drive from the Look in: drop-down menu (use the down arrow next to the box). Then hold the Shift key, and choose up to 20 .htm files to transfer. (Remember you need to send your graphics and sounds separately from the text files.) Click on Upload Files, and away they go to the Geocities server. Continue doing this until all of your files have been uploaded. It's as easy as that!

Go!

Once you have uploaded your pages, your site is ready for the world to see. It can be viewed by anyone who knows your Web address, but there are billions who won't know about your Web site. Sometimes this is a good thing. You don't always feel comfortable having strangers look at your personal Web pages. If that's the case, then just send out an e-mail to your friends and family telling them your new Web address.

However, sometimes you do want lots of people to see your site—especially if it's an informational site. If you want to announce your site to the world, then it's time to list with a search engine.

Search engines are software programs that use robots to search through lists of pages on the Web. When you put your Web address on the list, the robots can easily find your page. Your site is put into a group with other pages like it. That way, it's easier for people to find.

A viewer will come to the search engine and type in some words about what they're looking for (called keywords). The search engine sends the robot on a

MEMORY CHECK

Remember to choose ASCII for text files and BINARY for images and sounds.

mission to find sites that have those words. You need to help by putting some keywords into your code. It's time to hit the code again! This time, you need to put in a new tag called **<META>**.

The **<META>** tag is put in the **<HEAD>** section. It doesn't need a closing tag. The **<META>** tag has two attributes. The **NAME** attribute shows the type of action that the tag will do. If you put **="Keywords"** after the attribute, the computer will know that's what the **<META>** tag is for. The search engine robot will know to look there for keywords.

The **CONTENT** attribute then has all of the keywords that you want to use to describe your site. Put commas between each word so that the robot knows to read each one separately. Write just about any word that you think people might look for. If you were creating a joke site, for example, your tags might look like this:

<HTML>

<HEAD>

<TITLE>Now That's Funny!</TITLE>

<META NAME="Keywords" CONTENT="comedy, funny, laughter, puns, jokes, riddles, knock-knock, humor, ha ha, laughing, chuckle, guffaw, smile, silly, fun, funny bone, snicker, tee hee, hee hee, sense of humor, funniest, funnier, humorous, jest, slaphappy, hysterical, happy, comic"

</HEAD>

</HTML>

Use your imagination when you are thinking up keywords. This is how people are going to find you on the search engine. Use any words that you can think of that are related to your site.

You're not done with the new tags yet. Now that the search engine knows when to pull up your site, you need to tell the search-engine users what your site is about. As soon as the search engine finds all of the correct sites, it puts them into a list for the viewer. The list also shows a short description of the site. That way, the viewer can tell if he or she wants to visit.

It's time for another **<META>** tag. This time, instead of **="Keyword,"** type in **="Description"** next to the **NAME** attribute. Now the robot will know what you want to say about your site. Use a **CONTENT** attribute, and type in what your Web site is about.

<HTML>

<HEAD>

<TITLE>Now That's Funny!**</TITLE>**

<META NAME="Description" CONTENT="Cornelia's Comedy Corner is a site devoted to those who love rib-tickling humor. If you're ready to laugh your funny bone off, then this site is for you! It's full of jokes, riddles, and puns.">

</HEAD>

</HTML>

So now you're all tagged up and ready to be listed on the search engines. But wait! How do you tell the search engine that you want to be listed?

You have to visit the sites where you want your page listed. Each has a link called Add Page or Submit a Site or something like that. The link has directions on how to be listed.

Don't expect to see your listing right away. It may take a few weeks. This varies, so keep checking to see if it's on there.

TECHNO TIP

Keep it simple! Your description should be short. Otherwise, some search engines won't list it on their sites. In fact, some search engines only let you use a certain number of words. Just remember to say what is most important about your site.

Resources

You've Been Tagged!

Wow! There have been so many tags and so much to learn. Your head's probably swimming with tags by now. But don't worry if you don't remember it all. Here's a handy list of all the tags. You can just turn here whenever you need a quick reminder. This section lists all of the basic opening and closing tags. Read on to see a list of the attributes as well.

THE TAGS

Opening	Closing	Purpose
<HTML>	</HTML>	These must open and close all code for Web pages.
<HEAD>	</HEAD>	These open and close the page's <HEAD> section.
<TITLE>	</TITLE>	These hold the page's title, which will show up in the browser's top bar.
<BODY>	</BODY>	These open and close the main section of the page. (Anything you type between these tags will show up on the screen.)
<H1>	</H1>	
<H2>	</H2>	
<H3>	</H3>	
<H4>	</H4>	
<H5>	</H5>	
<H6>	</H6>	

<H7>	**</H7>**	These heading tags increase or decrease the size of the type that's between them (H1 is the largest; H7 is the smallest.)
<P>	**</P>**	The paragraph tags put spaces between lines of text.
** **	None	The break tag also puts a space between lines of text, but it's smaller than the paragraph tag space.
<HR>	**</HR>**	These tags add a home rule (or line) that makes a dividing line across the page.
<FONT>	**</FONT>**	These tags set the font of your text.
<B>	**</B>**	These tags make the text between them bold.
<I>	**</I>**	These tags make the text between them italic.
<U>	**</U>**	These underline all text that's between them.
<STRIKE>	**</STRIKE>**	These tags put a line through the middle of the text between them (as if they're crossed out).
<BLINK>	**</BLINK>**	These make the text between them blink on and off.
^{	**}**	These tags raise the text between them above the line (needed for words like 1st).
_{	**}**	These tags lower the text between

		them below the line (needed for words like H_2O).
<IMG>	None	The image tag inserts your pictures on the page. It's used with .gif or .jpg extensions
<A>	</A>	The anchor tags are used for setting up hyperlinks.
<TABLE>	</TABLE>	These tags create a table or box to let you organize your information.
<TR>	</TR>	These tags begin and end each row in a table.
<TD>	</TD>	These tags begin and end each cell in a table row.
<FORM>	</FORM>	These create fill-in forms on your page.
<INPUT>	None	This form tag is used to create a space for viewers to put information.
<SELECT>	</SELECT>	These form tags are used to create a selection box.
<OPTION>	None	This lists the name of the option in the selection box.
<FRAMESET>	</FRAMESET>	These create a set of frames on a page.
<FRAME>	None	This makes a specific section or frame inside of a frameset.
<UL>	</UL>	These create a bulleted list.
<OL>	</OL>	These create a numbered list.

<LI>	None	Use this to begin a line of text in a numbered or bulleted list.
<!--	**//-->**	The comments tags hold information that you don't want the viewer to see, such as reminder notes or instructions you want to remember. The viewer can't see any text that's between these tags.
<MARQUEE>	**</MARQUEE>**	These tags will scroll your text across the page.
<META>	None	This is used to create keywords that describe your site to search engines.

THE ATTRIBUTES

Just one reminder: Don't forget to put all of the words you list for the attributes inside of quotation marks, such as NAME="Happy".

BACKGROUND=	This lets you put in an image.
BGCOLOR=	This lets you add a color to the background.
BGSOUND=	This adds sound to the page.
ALIGN=	You can tell the computer to put something left, right, or center.
SIZE=	This decides the size of an object. It can be width, height, or both.
WIDTH=	This shows how far across the screen the object should go.
HEIGHT=	This shows how tall the object will be.
NOSHADE=	Rules are normally three-dimensional. This option turns it into a flat line.

COLOR=   This sets the color of an object.

SRC=   This is the source tag. It lists the location of where to find your file.

ALT=   This is the text that you include to display in case an image can't be shown.

HREF=   This tells the location and name of a file you want to link. It is used as an external link and will jump to another page. Use .htm/.html extensions only.

NAME=   This is the name of an object.

BORDER=   This is used to determine the color or size of a border.

CELLSPACING=   This determines the space between the cells.

ACTION=   This gives the instruction of where the information on a form is to be sent.

METHOD=   This explains what a form should do. For example, **METHOD="post"** means to send information.

TYPE=   This tells what kind of space to provide: text, radio, checkbox, submit, or clear.

VALUE=   This determines more specifically what the object is.

ROWS=   This determines the size each row inside a frameset will be.

COLS=   This determines the size each column inside a frameset will be.

TARGET=   The name of the frame section where images, pages, or links will show up once they're clicked.

CONTENT= The words or description that summarize what a Web site is about. It is for search engines to use.

A Symbol-ic Gesture

HTML uses lots of symbols, such as the ampersand (&), in its code. So what do you do when you have to use an ampersand in your text? If you try to just type it in, it won't show up on your page, and you might confuse your computer. You have to use a special code to create the symbols on your page. Below are some of the most common symbols and their codes. You just type the code in wherever you need the symbol.

Symbol	Code
&	&
"	"
@	@
#	#
©	©
®	®
™	™
$	$
¢	¢
%	‰
á	á

Coloring Your World

There are 16 color names that the Web recognizes. You can just type the names of these colors in whenever you need them. They are silver, grey, maroon, navy, black, teal, purple, olive, green, blue, magenta, cyan, yellow, lime, red, and white. The rest are written in hexadecimals (hek-zuh-DE-si-muhls). The hexadecimal color system uses the letters C and F and the numbers 0, 3, 6, and 9. The numbers and letters are a code that tells the computers what colors to show.

Have you ever mixed two different paints together and come up with a different color? That's sort of how the hexadecimal system works. Each hexadecimal code has six symbols. The first two are how much red will be in the color. The second two show how much green will be in the color. The last two show how much blue there will be. The number 0 is the darkest shade of any of those colors. The letter F is the lightest. If you wanted lots of dark blue in a color, you would put 00 in the last two spaces of the code. See the chart for more examples.

You don't have to use just these, though. They're only a small sample of what's available. Try experimenting with different combinations to find colors you like. There are only two things you have to do: You have to put a # sign before the code, and you have to have six digits in the code.

General Troubleshooting

There are some things you can check in your code if you're having problems. Take a good look for the following:

- When you opened a tag, did you close it?
- Did you check the typing and spelling of tags?
- Did you check to see if both brackets are there?
- Did you use the equal sign and quotation marks in attributes?
- Are your tags nested in the proper order, with one set of opening and closing tags inside of another?

HEXACHROME COLOR CHART

#FFFFFF	#FFFFCC	#FFFF99	#FFFF66	#FFFF33
#FFFF00	#FFCC00	#FFCC99	#FFCC66	#FFCC00
#FF9933	#FF9900	#FF6633	#FF6600	#FF0000
#FF9999	#FF6699	#FF3399	#FF33CC	#FF66CC
#CC99CC	#CC66CC	#993399	#996699	#999999
#6666CC	#9999FF	#6363C6	#0096C6	#093093
#C6FFF6	#C3C6CF	#30C6C6	#6363C6	#006393
#99FFFF	#99FFCC	#669999	#003939	#093909
#9966CC	#99CC33	#99CC00	#66FF33	#9C9339
#F6FFCF	#C6FF9C	#99CC30	#966336	#6C6C30
#996600	#CC9966	#C66330	#9C3909	#930000
#CC6600	#996633	#933C09	#663333	#630000
#333333	#999999	#F0F0F0	#CFCFCF	#CCCCCC
#666666	#909090	#606060	#303030	#000000

The FAQ Zone

Many Web sites have a Frequently Asked Questions (or FAQ) page. This page answers a lot of the common questions that viewers have about the site. That way, the viewer doesn't have to search around or e-mail the Webmaster to find out a simple answer.

Learning HTML takes time and practice. In fact, it takes lots. And it may not feel like it at first, but you learn a lot from making mistakes. The FAQ Zone section is here to give answers to common questions about building a Web page. Maybe you will see one of your questions here.

I typed the first part of the heading and the body in the document, but when I view it in the browser nothing shows up.

This is the most common question. There are several things to check. First, look at your code. Do you have all of the opening and closing tags? Check especially for the **<HTML>** and **</HTML>** tags. Also check the spelling. It's easy to accidentally type in **<HTLM>**.

Next, check to see if you saved your document as an .htm (or .html) file. If your file name is Index.txt, then you have a text file and not an HTML file. You will need to rename it Index.htm. Right-click on the icon that shows up on the floppy disk, and choose Rename from the menu that appears. Type in the new file name. You could also reopen the file and choose Save As to save the file with the correct name. You will then have two files, so you will need to delete the Index.txt file. On a Macintosh, you can just type over the old name with the new name.

Finally, is the file you are looking for on your floppy, or is it saved somewhere else? It will still work as long as you tell the browser where the file is and the correct name of the file you wish to open.

I opened the Save As box to save my Web file. I know I saved it, but now I can't find it. Where is it?

Remember the box that contains the file name, where you typed in Index.htm? Look below it, and you will see another box called Files of type:. Click on the arrow next to it, and select All Files (*.*). Now you will be able to see your file on the disk. The computer automatically only shows .txt or .doc files. You have to tell it to show everything through the All Files option.

Help! All my type is blinking instead of just one word! (Or: My type is all blue, and I only wanted one sentence to be blue. Or: My type is HUGE!)

It really makes the page look nice when you make certain words look different. You do that by adding a heading, color, size, or style tag. But if the text from that point on all looks the same as the word you wanted to make different, then you know you forgot the closing tag. Or, sometimes you just forget to add a bracket, or you mistyped the closing tag. Go back to where the change begins, and look at the tags. Then look for the closing tag. If there is one, look to see that it has all the brackets and is spelled correctly.

I know I opened my browser and my text editor, but I can't find the browser now that I've been working in the text editor for a while.

If you do not see a small button for your browser on the task bar at the bottom of your screen, then you accidentally closed the browser program. Be careful to click the minus sign when you minimize a program. If you accidentally click on the X, it will close the entire program, and you will have to reopen it.

My lines on the page are all squished together. What went wrong?

You need to add the paragraph tags (**<P>** and **</P>**) before and after the text that you want to set apart from the rest. Use the **
** tag for a line break with a little less space.

I can't get the color to work on my page!

If you want background color, use the **BGCOLOR= ""** attribute inside of the **<BODY>** tag. Your code should look something like this: **<BODY BGCOLOR="Blue">** or **<BODY BGCOLOR="#0000FF">**. If you used one of the 16 predefined colors, check to see if you put the equal sign and quotation marks in the code. The quotation marks should go before and after the color. If you used a hexadecimal color, check to be sure that you put the # sign before the six-digit number. The hexadecimal should also be inside of quotation marks.

Why won't my image show up? I know I put it in the code.

Did you save the image as a .gif or .jpg file? You should also check to make sure you saved it on your floppy disk. Your images need to be in the same location as your Web files.

Also check to make sure that you put the correct tag in the code. The **<IMG>** tag should be in brackets with an **SRC** attribute. There should be brackets at both ends, and the **SRC** attribute needs to have an equal sign after it and then the file name in quotations. Make sure that the name of the image file is typed in correctly and exactly the same as it looks on the disk.

How do I position my picture?

You can use the **<CENTER>** and **</CENTER>** tags before and after the image tags to place your image in the middle of the page.

You also can use the **ALIGN** attribute to align the image to the left, right, or center of the page. The code would look like this: **<CENTER><IMG SRC="image.gif"></CENTER>** or **<IMG ALIGN= "center" SRC="image.jpg">**.

My picture is way too big (or too small). How do I fix it?

Use the **HEIGHT** and **WIDTH** attributes with the **<IMG>** tag to change its size. Experiment to see how different sizes look on your page. And don't forget the equal sign and quotation marks with the attribute. The code would be like this: **<IMG SRC="image.gif" HEIGHT="100" WIDTH="50">**.

Resources for Webmasters (Like You!)
FREE GRAPHICS AND IMAGES
http://www.clipart.com

http://www.megago.com

http://www.freebieconnection.com

http://www.kidsdomain.com

http://www.free-backgrounds.com

http://webcavern.com/clipart

http://www.aplusart.com

http://www.doghouse.com

http://www.iconbazaar.com

http://www.animfactory.com

http://www.clipartguide.com

FREE GUEST BOOKS
http://www.bravenet.com

http://www.Guestpage.com

http://www.sitegadgets.com

http://www.dreambook.com

http://www.htmlgear.lycos.com

FREE PAGE COUNTERS

http://www.pagecount.com

http://www.ultimatecounter.com

ONLINE HELP WITH COLORS

http://www.wdvl.com/authoring/graphics/colour
(help with hexadecimal charts and color information)

http://www.geocities.com/siliconvalley/network/2397
(explains the hexadecimal chart)

http://www.hidaho.com/colorcenter/cc.html

ART SOFTWARE

PhotoShop: http://www.Adobe.com/photoshop

Paint Pro: http://www.Jasc.com/psp6.html

Corel Draw: http://www.Corel.com/draw9/index.htm

FREE JOKES & RIDDLES

http://www.riddlenut.com

http://www.bogglers.com

http://www.jokesgalore.com

FREE GAMES

http://www.funbrain.com

http://www.kidland.com

http://www.happypuppy.com

http://www.Javaonthebrain.com

FREE SOUNDS

http://www.Pagetalk.com

http://www.wavethemes.org

http://www.soundamerica.com

http://www.wavcentral.com

Must-See Sites on the Web

SEARCH ENGINES FOR KIDS

http://www.Yahooligans.com

http://www.AskJeevesforKids.com

http://www.dogpile.com

WEB SAFETY

http://www.vtw.org/pubs/ipcfaq

http://www.pearlsw.com

http://www.freezone.com

CLUBS AND ORGANIZATIONS FOR KIDS

Organizations: http://www.worldkids.net

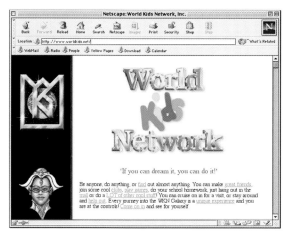

HTML Guild: http://www.HTML.com

Web License:
http://www.pbs.org/kids/did_you_know/did_techknow.html

COPYRIGHT INFORMATION
http://www.benedict.com

HANDY WEB TUTORIALS
http://www.hotwired.com/webmonkey/kids

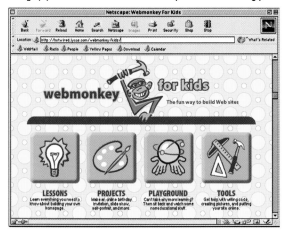

http://www.htmlgoodies.com/primers/basics.html

http://www.nashville.net/~carl/htmlguide/index.html

http://www.davesite.com

http://www.webdiner.com

http://www.reallybig.com

Web Hosting
GUIDES TO WEB HOSTS
http://www.hostreview.com

http://www.freewebspace.net

FREE WEB HOSTING
http://www.forfree.com

http://www.xoom.com

http://www.angelfire.com

http://www.Geocities.com/join/freehp.html

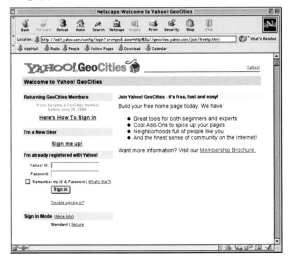

http://www.Prohosting.com

http://www.Spree.com

http://www.Tripod.com

http://www.useractive.com

GUIDE TO INTERNET SERVICE PROVIDERS
http://ispfinder.com

Programs for Web Designers
WEB AUTHORING PROGRAMS
http://www.Microsoft.com/FrontPage.com

http://www.Adobe.com/pagemill

http://www.Sausage.com

http://www.coffecup.com

http://www.allaire.com/products/homesite

http://www.Claris.com

http://www.miracleinc.com

FTP PROGRAMS
http://www.Ipswitch.com

Web Words

Acronym A way of shortening a long phrase by taking the first letter or letters of each of its words and creating a new word, such as taking **S**elf-**C**ontained **U**nderwater **B**reathing **A**pparatus and making it SCUBA.

Alignment Positioning an object so that it will be situated to the left, right, or center of your Web page.

Analog A series of voice transmissions. This is the format of information carried over telephone wires. In order for computers to read and understand it, they must use a modem to translate it into digital form.

ASCII American Standard Code for Information Interchange. This 128-character code uses letters, numbers, and symbols to create information that can be read on computers and over the Web.

Attribute This is a special tag that describes an HTML tag. It gives the computer specific instructions on how to display information.

Binary A series of number sequences that can be read by the computer to understand types of information.

Body The main part of your HTML Web page.

Browser A software program that allows a viewer to see a Web page on a computer that's connected to the Internet.

Clip art These are small pieces of artwork that you can use to help illustrate your page. You sometimes have to pay for the right to use them.

Code Letters, words, numbers, and symbols that make up a language understood by the computer. HTML is a type of code.

Content The information that's included on your Web page. It includes both text and graphics.

Copyright This is protection from the U.S. government that says what you create on your Web page belongs to you.

Cyber Anything that is related to the Internet or the Web.

Data Another word for information. This could be in the form of letters, numbers, words, or images.

Dialogue box The box that sometimes pops up when you click on an object on your hard drive. It will tell you what to do next.

Digital A series of digits or numbers that, when put together, creates a language the computer can read and understand.

Domain name A unique name for a Web site. It ends with an extension that identifies what type of page it is.

Download Electronically getting information, files, or programs from another computer and bringing them on to your computer.

Drop-down menu A menu of options that drops down from an object that you click on.

E-mail Electronic mail. This service allows the sending of messages and other mailed information over the Internet.

Extension The period and letters at the end of a domain name or file name. A domain name extension identifies what type of site it is, such as .edu for an educational institution. A file name extension identifies what type of file it is, such as .htm (or .html) for HTML documents.

FAQ Frequently Asked Questions. Used by many Web pages to give the answers to commonly asked questions.

Floppy disk The hard, plastic 3½-inch disk that is used in the A: drive on most computers.

Font The different size, shape, and style typefaces for text.

Formatting Arranging a Web page's information through changing the size, style, or color of its contents.

Forms These are interactive text boxes that a viewer can use to type information and send it to you using your e-mail.

Frames This is a way to divide a Web page so that a different Web document is shown in each section on the page.

FTP File Transfer Protocol. This is a software program that follows the rules for sending files or information over the Internet.

GIF Graphics Interchange Format. This is a type of file that is used to put pictures on a Web page. It reduces the size of the image and helps it load faster.

Heading The title or beginning of a document, which usually stands out from the rest of the text.

Hexadecimal A system of making colors in the computer using a series of the letters A through F and the numbers 0 through 9.

.htm/.html The extension used to save Web files. It tells the browser that it's a Web document so the browser will know how to show it.

HTML HyperText Markup Language. This is one of the main programming codes used to create Web pages.

Hyperlink A highlighted word or an icon on a Web page that connects the viewer to other Web pages.

Icon A small picture or object that is used to identify a program or company.

Image A general term for any object that displays as a picture.

Internet The network of computers and hardware connected by phone lines, wires, and satellite.

ISP Internet Service Provider. This is a company that connects your computer to the Internet through your modem and a phone or cable line.

JAVA Another type of Web programming language that's more advanced than HTML.

JavaScript Another type of Web programming language written in scripts that lets a Web page be more interactive.

JPEG Joint Photographic Expert Group. This is another type of file used to place pictures in a Web document. It also condenses the color in a picture and is used mainly for photographs.

Maximize To enlarge a computer window by selecting the symbol of double boxes in the upper right corner of the title bar at the top of the window.

Minimize To shrink down a computer window by selecting the minus symbol in the upper right corner of the title bar at the top of the window. The minimized window shows up as a button at the bottom of the screen.

Navigation How one moves from Web page to Web page by clicking on the hyperlinks.

Notepad This is the name of the text editor that can be found on a PC.

Online The state in which a viewer is connected to the Internet using his or her service provider, computer, phone lines, and modem.

Password A secret word that you use to protect certain information, such as your e-mail. Never give this information out to anyone online.

Pixels These are the tiny dotlike fragments of color that are placed in rows across and down your computer screen. When they all merge together, they display images on your screen.

Pop-up menu A list of options that will automatically appear on your screen when you click on a certain object.

Publish This is how you let the world see your Web page. When you have finished creating and testing your page, you will send it to a server computer, and it will be displayed on the Web for all to see.

Refresh This means to update. You will need to do this to your page when you make changes to your .htm files and want to see the new design.

Search engine An online software program that is designed to look up information on the Web.

SimpleText The name of the text editor that can be found on a Macintosh computer.

Source The location of an object.

Table A boxlike structure that is used to put information together in an organized manner on your Web page. It is also used to position objects and text on a page.

Tags All HTML code that is placed inside of angle brackets (< >). There are usually both opening and closing tags.

Text editor This is a simple word processing program that allows you to make Web page documents.

Upload Sending information, files, or programs from your computer to another computer.

URL Uniform Resource Locator. The address of a Web page.

View source A way to look at the code of any Web page by right-clicking or clicking and holding on the page. (Also called page source.)

Virus This is a computer bug you can get from downloading .exe or .com files. It can cause serious damage to your computer.

Web host provider A company that owns or operates a server computer that is used to store Web pages.

Web page A document that can be viewed on a computer connected to the Internet.

Web site A Web page and its address.

World Wide Web A collection of all of the pages made through coded programming that can be viewed by Internet hardware.

Index

My Pals' Web Pages

....

....

....

....

....

....

....

....

....

....

....

Webmaster Resources

Awesome Web Sites

....

....

....

....

....

....

....

....

....

....

....

....

....